To Suzanne, my life partner

An American in Persia

RICHARD A. KAUFFMAN

An American in Persia

A PILGRIMAGE TO IRAN

Foreword by Arli Klassen

Cascadia
Publishing House
Telford, Pennsylvania

Cascadia Publishing House LLC orders, information, reprint permissions:
contact@cascadiapublishinghouse.com
1-215-723-9125
126 Klingerman Road, Telford PA 18969
www.CascadiaPublishingHouse.com

An American in Persia
Copyright © 2010 by Cascadia Publishing House
a division of Cascadia Publishing House LLC, Telford, PA 18969
All rights reserved.
Library of Congress Catalog Number: 2009053800
ISBN 13: 978-1-931038-75-1; **ISBN 10:** 1-931038-75-9
Book design by Cascadia Publishing House
Cover design by Merrill R. Miller
Cover and interior photos by Richard A. Kauffman

The paper used in this publication is recycled and meets the
minimum requirements of American National Standard for Information Sciences—Permanence of Paper for Printed Library Materials, ANSI Z39.48-1984.

Library of Congress Cataloguing-in-Publication Data
Kauffman, Richard A.
An American in Persia : a pilgrimage to Iran / Richard A. Kauffman ; foreword by
Arli Klassen.
  p. cm.
Summary: "Kauffman tells stories of his encounters with Iranians, their culture,
and politics, to give witness to ways walls can break down when the stories, culture,
and history of others are attended to"--Provided by publisher.
Includes bibliographical references.
ISBN-13: 978-1-931038-75-1 (5.5 x 8.5" trade pbk. : alk. paper)
ISBN-10: 1-931038-75-9 (5.5 x 8.5" trade pbk. : alk. paper)
1. Iran--Description and travel. 2. Kauffman, Richard A.--Travel--Iran. 3. Americans--Travel--Iran. 4. Mennonites--Travel--Iran. 5. Intercultural communication--Iran--Case studies. 6. Iran--Social life and customs. 7. Iran--Politics and government--1997- 8. Politics and culture--Iran. I. Title.

DS318.9.K38 2010
955.06'1--dc22

                                        2009053800

        17 16 15 13 12 11 10   10 9 8 7 6 5 4 3 2 1

Contents

Iran and its neighbors. Map taken from the CIA World
Factbook *in public domain. https://www.cia.gov/library/
publications/the-world-factbook/maps/maptemplate_ir.html*

Foreword

"Welcome to Iran. It is so good to have you visiting us." This is the welcome to foreigners, especially Americans—on the street and in the bazaars, in city after city, throughout Iran. People constantly come up to the foreigners, first to ask them where they are from, and then to welcome them to Iran. At first this experience is scary, and then with time it becomes an astonishing commentary from the people of Iran about their desire for peaceful relations with the people of America.

Formal diplomatic relations between the United States and Iran have been severed since 1979. Belligerence and hostility emanate from the governments of both countries. Both accuse the other of failure to abide by various international agreements, and both are correct. How might there begin to be peaceful relations between these two countries? How might the church be involved in peacebuilding work between countries who have each declared the other to be their enemy? Why should the church be involved?

Mennonite Christians take seriously Jesus' call to "love our enemies," and to "do good to those who hate you." Mennonite Central Committee (MCC) is the worldwide ministry of Anabaptist churches, sharing God's love for all in the name of Christ, by responding to basic human needs and working for peace and justice. MCC has a presence in sixty-five countries around the world. As Richard Kauffman explains, MCC has been working at "track two diplomacy," people-to-people relationships in Iran, since 1990. This includes sending some ten delegations to visit Iran and its people, to experience first-hand their hospitable welcome, and to break down stereotypes about Americans and Iranians (who are mostly Persian, not Arab). I participated in one of these visits in 2007, and Richard Kauffman made the trip in 2008.

This is Richard's story of his experience in Iran. His story is very similar to the stories from all of us who have participated in this kind of peacemaking travel. And yet, his story is his alone, through his eyes, as his own reflections on his experience. At MCC we have encouraged participants to tell their stories—to help others to experience Iran as they experienced Iran, and to engage in discussion where there are differences of understanding and interpretation. We expect that this book will do exactly that—draw you in to Richard's experience of Iran, and to open up questions and discussions about things that surprise you, or even anger you.

This is peacebuilding work on a people-to-people basis, something which we believe the church is called to do. There are some in the Christian West who see this peacebuilding work as far too political. And, there are others in the political realm who see this peacebuilding work as far too naïve. Both are valid criticisms.

And yet, it is precisely because the church, and in particular Mennonite churches, are separate from the government, that there is opportunity to open the door to relationships that are not based on enmity or hostility, while debating differences in worldviews and belief. There has been much discussion about these differences! It is only in understanding where there is similarity, and where there is difference, that mutual trust and respect can begin.

Jesus asks us to love God, to love our neighbor, and to love our enemy. Richard's experience in Iran is a good story of how to do all three. May his experience inspire you to find creative ways to do the same.

—Arli Klassen, Executive Director
Mennonite Central Committee
Akron, Pennsylvania
www.mcc.org

The walls around the former United States' embassy in Tehran are still covered with anti-American slogans.

Introduction

In 1979 at the height of the Islamic Revolution in Iran, student radicals took hostage the diplomats and other personnel serving in the American embassy in Tehran and held them for 444 days. This crisis marked the end of diplomatic relations between the United States and Iran.

Currently, relationships between the two countries are quite hostile. Iran is supposedly working to develop nuclear weapons despite sanctions placed upon them by the United States, other Western countries, and the United Nations. The U.S. accuses Iran of supporting so-called terrorist groups like Hezbollah in Lebanon, Hamas in Palestinian territories, and radical Shiite groups in Iraq. There has been speculation that the U.S.—or Israel—might take military action against Iran, either to knock out their nuclear capabilities or to destroy weapons that purportedly are destined for Iraq to supply insurgents fighting against the U.S. military.

Occasionally, when governments won't talk with each other, opportunities open up for citizens to establish direct communication and engage in a cultural exchange. Political scientists call this people-to-people diplomacy.

One such opportunity came my way in January 2008, when I took a two-week "learning tour" in Iran sponsored by the Mennonite Central Committee (MCC), a religious relief, development, and peacemaking organization. The purpose of the tour was to learn about the history and culture, religion and politics of Iran and to attempt to build bridges between Iranians and Americans, Christians and Muslims. We met with government officials and university students in Tehran, university professors in Shiraz, and Islamic clerics and teachers in the holy city of Qom. We talked with people in the streets everywhere, including the ancient city of Esfahan.

There is a saying that if you go to Iran for a month you'll write a book; stay six months and you'll write an article; but if you stay a year you won't write anything. The more you know, the more you realize you don't know. So it's a bit audacious of me to have been there but two weeks and then write a book about Iran.

It needs to be said up front: I am not an authority on Iran. Whenever I found myself trying to pose as an authority while writing this book, I felt like I had gotten off track and had to get back on it again. There are many other books you should read if you want an authoritative picture of modern-day Iran or of the Persian Empire (see the resources section). My intention is to serve as witness, to give a testimony of what I saw and heard and learned and experienced while in Iran. Indeed, I was on a spiritual pilgrimage, and in many ways it was transformative.

What lies ahead, then, if you have the courage to proceed, are many stories and observations about Iran. Before I get to the stories, however, I want to share some reflections about cross-cultural encounters: what happens when we cross boundaries between cultures, peoples, nations, and religions. If this more theoretical stuff doesn't interest you, skip it and move directly to the first chapter.

On one of our first days in Iran our MCC learning tour group had an interesting conversation about how we "see" Iran. Wally Shellenberger, one of our tour leaders, encouraged us to look for the good in Iran, not the bad. All learning does involve some measure of suspending our own judgment. For when we prejudge things we can be blinded to things as they really are. And while I certainly wanted to see the good in Iran, I responded that I wanted to see things "whole," that is, get a more complete picture. We need to get beyond the demonizing of Iran that the U.S. engages in. Yet I'm not sure it is even in the best interests of the people of Iran if we only see and report on the positive things in their history and culture.

I was speaking, in part, as a journalist: I identified with the goals of the MCC learning tour—to learn about Iran and begin to build bridges with the people of Iran. But I also was being sent by *The Christian Century* with the expectation that I would write something about Iran for the magazine.[1] I had my editor's perspective in mind: He is a realist in political matters, and I knew he wouldn't accept anything that painted only a rosy picture of Iran.

One extreme in cross-cultural encounters is to become so infatuated with the new and novel that one romanticizes it, overlooking its flaws and dark sides. There is a long history of this response, particularly from Western intellectuals, artists, and writers who for the first time are exposed to Eastern culture. They can be so enthralled with the mysterious cultures of the East that they come to believe that the sun both rises on and sets on the East.

This fascination with a culture different from one's own can be a way of rebelling against one's own culture, throwing off the strictures and mores and even the strengths of one's own culture and native land. For Americans traveling abroad who know what kind of mischief our government has done around the world, including in Iran, it is easy to think that nothing good comes out of the United States, whereas the reality is much more complex than that.

The other more dominant tendency in cross-cultural encounters is to find the "Other" so strange or even threatening that we demonize it. We know all about that, given the chatter in the West since 9-11 about the clash of civilizations between the West and the Muslim East and the so-called "war on terrorism." This "war" is essentially a battle to wipe out extremist Islam without ever really come to terms with it or learning to know what motivates it. Remember in the build up to the 2003 Iraq War, even the president of the United States didn't know the difference between Sunni and Shi'a Islam. He thought they were all just "Muslims," which is like glossing over the difference between Catholic, Orthodox, and Protestant Christians.

We humans have the tendency to conscript others and the reality of their lives into our own conception of reality.[2] Think of Christians' views of Jews over the years: They have been viewed as Christ killers, pharisaical legalists, power-grabbing, money-loving materialists. The role they have played in our own stories may have little to do with reality, and certainly Jews often don't recognize themselves or their history in what we claim about them.

Of course what is typically at work here is projection at best or scapegoating at worst. We project our own fears and anxieties onto other people and cultures or we blame them for our own problems. They become a symbol of what threatens us. This is not to say that others don't represent a real threat to us: think al Qaeda, for instance. But both real and perceived threats can blind us to reality, and as a consequence we can take actions not necessarily in our own best interests, much less that of others. The preemptive Iraq War is a prime example of that.

In the current political environment, especially after 9-11, all Muslims can be painted with the same brush: They are viewed as terrorists or at least Islamic extremists. People who look Middle Eastern are "profiled" and therefore deemed suspect. As I first wrote this, there was news about several Muslim families thrown off a domestic U.S. flight just because someone else heard them say something that sounded suspicious, when apparently the families were having a benign conversation about which part of the plane is the safest in case of an accident.

It is not possible to see others objectively. God alone has a full picture of reality, but even God doesn't see things from a disinterested or objective perspective, since God loves all creation and wishes to be in relationship with it. While we can't step outside our own perspective, there are ways in which we can learn to see things from others' perspective. Certainly travel is one of those ways—encountering another culture, meeting the people, listening to their stories, learning their history, seeing their art, hearing their music, eating their food, receiving their perspective on the world, not least their perceptions of us and their relationship with us. And that is what happened on this learning tour to Iran.

Miroslav Volf suggests that to come to better understanding of other people we need what he calls "double vision."[3] This is an attempt to see others both from our own perspective and context and from theirs. This double vision requires four steps: First, we need to step outside ourselves and be prepared to be suspicious of our own perspectives on others. There is always the likely possibility that our views of them might be mere prejudice. At the same time, we need to be suspicious of our perspective on ourselves: we most likely have deceptive and exalted views of our own selves, history, and stories.

Second, we have to cross over a social boundary and move into the context of the other. Think of it as trying to put one's self into the skins of others, to see the world from their perspective. It doesn't mean that we have to accept that perspective but does calls us at least to come to understand it somewhat and even have some appreciation for it—at the very least to grasp the reasons for it, whether right or wrong.

Third, we have to take "the other" into our own world, says Volf. This is a means of comparing their perspectives with ours, not necessarily to reject either, but to see the two side by side. It may just be that we'll come to see both perspectives as wanting in some fashion and therefore in need of modification if not transformation.

Finally, because our perspective on others can never be fully complete, accurate, or even truthful, we have to start the process all over again. We must repeatedly step outside ourselves, moving into the social world of others, and imaginatively at least bringing their world and worldview into relationship with our own.

Aiming toward greater understanding and truthfulness about the other is an imperative of the commandment about not bearing false witness to one's neighbor. When our learning tour group left for Iran, the United States was amid a spirited political campaign, the 2008 presidential primaries. It seemed to me that many of the candidates, in trying to paint a negative image of their opponents, were guilty of violating the commandment against bearing false witness against their neighbor, in this case their political opponents. Our reputation is one of our most treasured "belongings," and when another person destroys it or takes it away from us, our lives can be destroyed as a result.

Think about what happens to a person who is falsely accused of child abuse, for example. His life may never be the same again. So the commandment against bearing false witness is a serious one, the counterpart to not murdering another person. Either way, we can destroy another, one way with words, the other with lethal weapons. In any case, it is my solemn obligation to not knowingly bear false witness against Iranians, their culture, their history, or even their infamous leaders, including President Ahmadinejad.

Yet truth-telling is important too, and the truth, especially for politicians, is not always welcome. I'm no more interested in protecting Ahmadinejad from the truth than I am leaders of my own country, although it is also imperative for me to try to understand why leaders take the positions they do. But of course truth-telling is always from our perspective. There are always two sides to every story, they say. My aim, therefore, was to try to see and hear all I could and then bear witness to what I had experienced in Iran.

Nevertheless, I am but one person. And I have my own limitations and perspectives. I did have the advantage of traveling with a group. We each saw different things, asked different questions of our Iranian hosts, and had our own interpretations. That meant I was privileged to see Iran through more than my one pair of eyes and ears. I especially benefitted from having Wally and Evie Shellenberger, who have spent three years in Iran in MCC's student exchange program, as our leaders and guides. I learned much more and "saw" more from traveling with these companions than if I had been alone.

Of course any factual errors or misinterpretations can not be blamed on my fellow travelers. For those I alone am culpable.

—*Richard A. Kauffman*
  Glen Elyn, Illinois

An American
in Persia

A protester at a rally in New York City when President Ahmadinejad addressed an interreligious group in fall 2008, a meeting co-sponsored by Mennonite Central Committee.

1 Getting oriented

Our trip to Iran began in Kitchener, Ontario, where the group convened for two half days of orientation. The major reason for holding the orientation in Ontario was to meet an Iranian family, the Daneshvars, who are in Canada as part of Mennonite Central Committee's student exchange program. While all the Mennonites who have gone to study in Iran have come from the United States, the Iranians who come this way have to study in Canada, since Iranians have difficulty getting visas for the U.S.

Mr. Daneshvar is studying theology at the Toronto School of Theology—a very Christian place for a Shi'a Muslim to study. He's working on a dissertation comparing Karl Barth and a twentieth-century Iranian theologian, both of whom are committed to a non-reductionistic view of their respective faiths. I didn't expect to get into a discussion of Barthian theology during an orientation for a trip to Iran, but that's what happened over a meal with Mr. Daneshvar. Mrs. Daneshvar is working at an industrial plant that assembles Blackberries. And their two children went to Rockway Mennonite Collegiate (a high school) when they first came to Canada; now they're students at the University of Waterloo.

What was particularly fascinating was to watch the interaction between the father and his young adult children. It was clear that he wanted to serve as the spokesperson for the family.

But the children couldn't help breaking in—good naturedly—
to challenge some of his interpretations about life back home in
Iran. The mother mostly sat quietly, sometimes with pained
looks on her face, when her husband and children were at odds
with each other. But she did speak when spoken to. And over a
meal the men and women ate separately, typical of mixed company in Iran. In that setting the women in our group said Mrs.
Daneshvar spoke freely. She and her daughter prepared the
women for how to wear the hijab and dress otherwise, as well as
how to conduct themselves as women in Iran. No hand-shak-
ing with men, for instance.

Over dinner I asked the young man how he felt when President Bush lumped his country in with the "axis of evil." With
firm resolve, he said that he knows his country and he knows
who he is, and that his image of both was not changed by President Bush's characterization of Iran. But then he added that he
knows who the evil one is, the Great Satan (that is, the United
States), echoing the language of the late Ayatollah Khomeini.
Power corrupts, he said, and since the U.S. is the most powerful
country in the world, it is the most corrupt country! I could
imagine most Americans taking great offense at his view of the
U.S. But I could see myself saying something similar, especially
if I were in his shoes.

I asked the family what they thought of President Ahmadinejad. He's a simple man, Mr. Daneshvar said, not sophis-
ticated enough to speak diplomatically. He should check his
rhetoric with people who are wiser in such matters than he is.
Nevertheless, Mr. Daneshvar said the president is a devout
Muslim and his religious utterances are sincere. While mildly
critical of Ahmadinejad, Mr. Daneshvar emphatically defended
his president's stance on Israel. The Holocaust really did happen, yet probably the number of Jews executed was more in the
thousands than millions. Besides, though it was horrendous
and shouldn't happen again, it took place in a Western country,
so why should people in the Middle East (the Palestinians) have
to pay for it?

An Anti-Arab sentiment was expressed also by this family, which is somewhat typical of Iranians, reflecting long suspicions between Persians and Arabs. This was especially true of the young man. I asked why he doesn't like the Arabs, and chief among his reasons was a stereotype you also hear in the West: You can't trust them. They say one thing, they do another.

The Dashevars had already been in Canada since 1998, so I assumed they had become rather assimilated to a Western culture, especially the young people. I asked them what they thought their biggest challenge was going to be adjusting back to Iranian culture when they return after the father completes his doctorate. The daughter said she didn't look forward to the heat in Iran, and the father said the traffic would bother him. It seemed like a naïve response; the reverse culture shock they will experience, especially the young people, will be more unsettling than something as superficial as weather or traffic.

In addition to meeting with the Dashevars, the other reason for meeting in Ontario was so that we could fly out of Toronto. The rationale was that, given the hostile relationships between the U.S. and Iran, it would be easier for us to fly from Canada. But ironically, when we flew back into Canada and went through U.S. customs, not a word was said or a question asked about my having just spent two weeks in Iran. The customs official didn't even pause to look at the Iranian stamp in my passport.

A chance meeting with Dr. Mohammad Hassan Ghadiri Abyaneh, an Iranian ambassador, led to a vigorous discussion about relations between Iran and the U.S.

2 Over the Mediterranean

On my flight from Frankfurt, Germany, to Tehran, Iran, the man in the seat next to me was unusually fidgety. Though he wasn't that large, he draped his arm over the armrest between us and to my great irritation elbowed me in my side from time to time. And at times he would even spread his legs apart and rest his left leg against my right one.

When our dinner was served, I thought it was time to learn to know this man. I introduced myself, saying that I was going to Iran for a two-week learning tour sponsored by the Mennonite Central Committee, a relief, development, and peacebuilding non-governmental organization in the United States. There were twelve of us in our group, I told him, including our American leaders, a couple who had studied in Iran for three years on an educational and cultural exchange. I let him know that we were interested in building bridges between our two countries, since our two governments were at enmity with each, and between Christians and Muslims as well.

To my great surprise I learned the man sitting next to me in the economy coach was an Iranian ambassador! He took great interest in my reason for visiting his native country, saying his country wants peace between our two countries. Nevertheless, he was quick to add that Iran is prepared to defend its own country and interests.

I told the ambassador that I had been present the previous fall (2007) when President Ahmadinejad met with some religious leaders at the United Nations. The meeting that got most of the media attention took place the day before at Columbia University. While introducing the president from Iran, President Bollinger of Columbia used the occasion to sharply rebuke Ahmadinejad for his stances on Israel and the Holocaust. It seemed like a public humiliation, a very inhospitable and uncharitable act—one that certainly constrasts with the hospitality for which Iranians are known.

I told the ambassador that on the day following the infamous engagement at Columbia, MCC sponsored a meeting in a chapel across from the UN headquarters. Ahmadinejad was given a chance to address the mostly religious audience. Then religious leaders from North America were given an opportunity to respond. Although differences were aired in this meeting, Ahmadinejad was treated with respect.

I let my seatmate know that while I'm very supportive of the Palestinian cause and in no way defend Israel's oppression of Palestinians, I found some of his president's rhetoric troubling—especially the seeming denial of the magnitude of Jewish holocaust of Israel's right to statehood.

In response, the ambassador parroted his president's own words. While the Holocaust may have taken several hundreds of thousands of Jewish lives—no way were six million involved, he said, echoing Ahmadinejad's claims—it was a crime perpetuated by a Western country. So why should the Palestinians have to pay for the sins of the West? The only solution to the Middle Eastern problem is to turn the land back over to the Palestinians and let them return to their homelands.

He had no tolerance at all for a two-state solution to the Palestinian problem,[4] as the state of Israel has no legitimacy whatsoever. He also told me that the two bars on the Israeli flag stand for the Nile River to their west and the Euphrates River to their east and that Israel's intention is to take all the land between these landmarks.

I acknowledged his point about the sins of the West not being visited upon the Palestinians. Yet I said I didn't think it was possible to turn back the clock to 1948 before Israeli statehood, and there could be no solution to the Middle East problem until Israel's right to exist was recognized by the other major players.

Then I changed the subject: What about religious freedom in Iran? Again, the ambassador echoed President Ahmadinejad. Religious minorities in Iran do have rights. As proof, the ambassador pointed to the fact that all the traditional minority religions in the country have representation in their parliament, including Zoroastrians, Christians, and Jews. But what about the Bahai, I asked, knowing that they experience outright persecution in Iran. They're not a revealed religion, he countered; Iran only recognizes revealed religions. In my country, I responded, we don't make that judgment; in the United States you have the right to be wrong about religion.

The ambassador also took exception with my Christian pacifism. He raised all the classical quandaries that pacifists typically hear, upping the ante with each one: Wouldn't you kill an assailant to save your son? Wouldn't you be willing to kill one person to save 100 children? If you had the chance to stop someone from dropping a nuclear weapon on a city, wouldn't you do it even if it meant you had to kill the person?

I allowed that in each case I would try to prevent the larger harm, but my understanding of what it means to follow Jesus proscribes the use of lethal force. I also admitted that I couldn't predict what I would do in the heat of the moment and that many Christians would agree with him, not me. It became apparent that behind his questions was an Iranian sense of justice—protection of the weak and setting straight an injustice are crucial. But he couldn't wrap his mind around the concept of working at justice nonviolently.

I suggested to the ambassador that the problem between the U.S. and Iran had to do with oil. His solution was very simple: "We have oil; we sell you oil. You have planes; you sell us planes." It seemed all too simple to me.

While our conversation continued on a bit, by this time I was physically and mentally exhausted. I slouched down in my seat, feigned a nap, and thought that our arrival in Iran couldn't happen too soon. When we finally touched down at the Imam Khomeini International Airport south of Tehran, I breathed a sigh of relief. But the ambassador and I parted amicably: He asked if he could take my picture with his cell phone, and I returned the favor with my own camera. We exchanged business cards, and he welcomed me to his country.

Mr. Haghani, from the Imam Khomeini Education and Research Institute (IKERI) in the city of Qom, was our very capable and affable tour guide.

3 Reception

Getting into Iran didn't happen quickly, as we were to find out when we went through immigration services as the Khomeini airport. Arriving at 1:30 a.m., we were all quite sleepy from two days of travel from Canada through Germany, where we had a long layover enroute to Tehran. Once our passports were stamped, we were all taken to a desk where we were fingerprinted. We wondered if this was in retaliation for the U.S. fingerprinting foreign guests in the aftermath of 9-11.

Afterward, we were allowed to use the restrooms to wash off the ink. Then we waited and waited to get final clearance and to have our passports returned to us. But it didn't come, and we weren't told why. Finally, one of the immigration officials pointed to James Cooper's beard. James, one of our fellow travelers, belongs to a small, sectarian group called the "Old Brethren," and he wears a long, full beard, a plain, denim coat and a broad-brimmed hat. The immigration official wanted to know if James is Jewish! Briefly I too was called over to a desk. My name—Kauffman—must have caught their eye too, as it can be a Jewish name. Although communication was very poor, almost non-existent, one word was clear: "deport." Were they aiming to deport James, if not me, for suspicion of being Jewish?

Finally, Evie Shellenberger, our one leader, was able to get the attention of Mr. Haghani, who served as our Iranian tour guide for our two-week visit. Dressed in his clerical robe and turban, he came into the immigration area. When he discovered why we were being detained, he told the immigration officials that "Mr. Cooper is Amish." Likely the immigration officials didn't know much about the Amish. But the critical point was made: neither James nor I are Jewish! We were soon released and sent on our way into the Tehran night, which was cold and snowy. At least the taxi cab I rode in had chains on its tires. The streets were not fit for travel. When we finally arrived at the Mashad Hotel and sorted out our luggage and room assignments, I fell into bed for a short night of sleep.

While we were held up in immigration, we were warmly welcome by the Iranian people themselves. From Tehran in the north, to Shiraz in the south and the cities of Qom, Kashan, and Esfahan in between, time and again individuals and groups would approach us on the street to ask us where we are from. At first I was reluctant to admit I was an American. But soon I learned that that was no problem.

A typical response was that Iranians don't have problems with the American people. It's just our government that they have a problem with. Some dared even to admit that their government is part of the problem. Several persons in very different parts of the country said President Ahmadinejad is just a kid—meaning, I think, that politically he is very unseasoned and immature. One man told me that their president needs to vet his public statements with more experienced politicians and diplomats.

The Iranians we met didn't see any reason why Iranians and Americans could not be friends. But they sometimes asked us difficult questions. While they seemed to give the American people some slack for President Bush's first term in office, we were asked why Americans voted him into office a second time. Some also dared to ask why Americans hate Iranians, or why Christians hate Muslims.

When we assured them we don't hate Iranians or Muslims, that we were visiting their country to send exactly the opposite message, some of them got misty-eyed. Most people we talked with were concerned that we would like their country and would get good impressions of it to take back home. There is an apparent disconnect between many Iranians and their government, at least when it comes to attitudes toward Americans.

One of the contradictions of Iranian society is that despite the fact woman have second-class status, sixty-five percent of university graduates are women.

4 A complicated country

Early on we met Nassrin (not her real name), a twenty-four-year-old. She had recently graduated from university with a degree in English literature. She was one of 3,000 students who had applied for one of twenty-five openings in a graduate program in English literature at the University of Tehran. She didn't make it the first time. While she wants to reapply again, she's also considering programs overseas, perhaps in the U. S. Canada, or Europe. She now works for an Iranian company about to launch a new web site to sell Iranian products worldwide. Nassrin had had a chance encounter with an earlier MCC learning tour, enjoyed getting to know its participants, and ever since has tried to spend a day with each group like ours.

Nassrin said to us, "Iran is a complex country. And so are the people." That became the mantra for the way we looked at and experienced this country with its ancient and rich culture and civilization.

Indeed the country is a complex place, as complex as a Persian rug. It is also a place of contradictions, the place where they grow sweet lemons and sour oranges, both of which are an acquired taste. Iran has a parliament and elections, but all candidates are vetted by a council controlled by the Islamic clerics who dominate the affairs of the country, and even the laws passed by Parliament have to be approved by this council. While women have second-class status, currently sixty-five percent of university graduates are women, to the consternation of the cleric-dominated government.

Iran has the third-largest supply of oil in the world and ample supplies of natural gas, yet it is also purportedly developing a nuclear energy program, to the consternation of Western governments. Keep in mind, though, that it was the American government, during the Shah of Iran's reign, which pressed upon Iran the need to develop a nuclear energy program in the eventuality that their oil would run out. (For more on the nuclear weapons issue, see David Cortright, p. 110.)

Everywhere we went in public places, Iran was using energy-conserving CFL light bulbs, yet they still burn leaded fuel and use pollution-spewing old cars without emissions controls. Gas is cheap, as you might expect in a country with a large supply of oil. It was running between forty and fifty cents while we were there. Cities like Tehran have a major pollution problem. In fact, we were forewarned that if any of us had an allergy problem, we should be sure to take our medicine with us. It was not uncommon to see locals wearing facemasks in Tehran.

Here might be the greatest contradiction of all: Iran is an Islamic Republic largely controlled by the Shi'a Muslim clerics. But only 1.4 percent of Iranians attend Friday prayers—the closest equivalent to Sunday morning worship in our context.[5] Nevertheless, Iran is a deeply religious place. After visiting the country in 2003, the German philosopher Jürgen Habermas said that in Iran even the atheists are spiritual!

Yes, Iran is a place of contradictions and contrasts, just like America. But Iran is not just a complex and contradictory country. It is also a very old country, with a rich and ancient tradition going back over 2,500 years,[6] yet it is now a very young country demographically. Ethnically, most of the people of Iran are Aryan in background. (Hitler's notion about the German people being an Aryan nation was a myth.)

Yet the country is ethnically diverse, with minority populations of Arabs, Turkic groups, Kurds, Armenians, and others. If one could do an "archaeological dig" of Iranian culture, one would find there at least five layers: ancient Persian culture, with elements of the traditional Zoroastrian religion; Shi'a Islamic culture, which has traditionally been reticent to have clerics run the government, although since the Safavid period (sixteenth–eighteenth centuries) clerics have functioned as advisors to the government; the radical Islamic culture which, since the Islamic Revolution of 1979, now runs the country. Some nomadic tribes still exist in Iran as well; and there are many people influenced by Western culture, especially professionals in the middle class.

At its zenith in 525 B.C. the Persian Empire reached from the Indus to the Nile River. King Cyrus II, whose grave we got to see, was the first great emperor of the Persian Empire. He is even remembered in the Old Testament for his benevolent liberation of the Jewish people from their captivity in Babylon in 539 B.C. and his authorization to rebuild the Jewish temple upon their return to their homeland (see 2 Chron. 36:22-23; Isa. 45:1-4).

Up until the eighteenth century, Iran was a capable rival to its neighboring Mogul and Ottoman empires and could relate as an equal to Western powers. But since then the country has been weak and susceptible to outside powers and influence (especially the Russians and British, but also the United States since World War II). Despite its ancient history, Iran is a young country demographically. A million people died in the Iran-Iraq War, about half of them in Iran. There is a missing generation as a result. A third of the population was under fifteen years of age in 2004.

Iran indeed has a rich culture. Hamid Dabashi, an Iranian who teaches at Columbia University, argues that the history of Iran is rooted more in its art, architecture, music, poetry, and philosophy than it is in the machinations of successive monarchs and dynasties.[7] While the economy is not its strength, education is highly valued. At the same time, the great brain drain of Iranian intellectuals emigrating to the West in recent decades has negatively impacted the country in many ways.

Philosophy, including Western philosophy, is very much valued. One professor of philosophy told us that the Islamic Revolution was not open to dialogue, but Iran's tradition of philosophy kept dialogue alive in the country. The same philosopher told us that if we want to know why Islamic extremism is growing in the world, we should read Friedrich Nietzche's *Will to Power* for the answer.

Iranians also greatly appreciate poetry. Their poets—figures like Hafez and Sa'di, the source of books by the German poet Goethe—are national heroes. (Rumi, incidentally, is not as adored in Iran as he is in America, where his popularity is attributed to Coleman Barks, an American poet who has promoted his work in the English-speaking world.) It is said that every Iranian home has at least two books: the Qur'an and a copy of Hafez's poetry, and there is a debate among some as to which book is more important.

The poet Hafez, born in AD 1320, lived during troubled times, just after Persia was overrun by the Mongol invaders. A sufi (that is, a mystic in the Muslim tradition), he used poetic verse to express love for God. Hafez, not his given name, means memorizer, since at a young age he committed the whole Qur'an to memory. He became more than just a poet, however; he was a philosopher who pondered the great mysteries of life and death, in subtle ways resisted authoritarian rulers, and still serves as a model for resisting authority in Iran.

Hafez also reflects something of the complexity of the Iranian "soul": a devout Muslim on the one hand, yet he could enjoy the pleasures of life. Wine is a favorite metaphor used in his poems. Here is one of his most popular verses:

> The wheel of fortune's sphere is a marvelous thing:
> What next proud head to the lowly dust will it bring?
> Tumult and bloody battle rage in the plain:
> Bring the blood-red wine and fill the goblet again![8]

While Farsi is the language of Iran, Arabic is their religious language, since it is the language of the Qur'an. Iranians claim their reading of the Qur'an is more lyrical than in Arabic-speaking countries, due to the influence of Iranian poetry.

The biggest hazard traveling in Iran was the air pollution and auto traffic in Tehran, which has one of the highest traffic fatality rates in the world.

5 Safe passage

I was anxious when anticipating going to Iran. I didn't feel threatened so much by what Iranians might do to me. Rather, I was afraid that my own country might bomb Iran while I was there. In response, I imagined radicals taking us hostage, a repeat performance of the hostage-taking incident in 1979.

But before we embarked for Iran the members of our tour group received some advice from one of our Iranian hosts: he encouraged us to think about our trip to Iran as a spiritual pilgrimage. And that resonated with me in two ways: that God would be with us along the way, and that God was already there, even in Shi'a Muslim Iran. Hence, I should entrust my anxieties to God, our traveling companion, and I should look for signs of the presence of God in Iran itself, rather than presume I was taking God to Iran.

Nowhere in Iran did our tour group feel threatened by the powers that be. While we did see some security personnel with automatic weapons in several of the cities, on the surface, at least, Iran did not seem like a very militaristic society, less so than say New York City since 9-11. We were in fact tickled by the fact—pun intended—that several places featherdusters were used for crowd control.

The only threat we experienced was the traffic, especially in Tehran. Red lights didn't seem to mean much, stop signs nothing at all, and crossing streets as a pedestrian seemed more risky than the Israelites crossing the Red Sea. At least divine intervention was welcome whenever we crossed a street.

While we never felt threatened by the authorities, it was unsettling to walk past the former American Embassy where the hostages were taken in 1979 and held for 444 days. The embassy walls are covered with anti-American signs and slogans, signs that are clearly not left over from the days of the embassy takeover but have been freshened up much more recently. The slogans are in both Farsi and English. "We will make American face a severe defeat," says one, and another says, "Under God's grace we shall give in against the dictatorship of no government, even the United States and other superpowers."

We had been forewarned to not take pictures of the embassy, which has been taken over by the department of mines. Some Iranians are particularly sensitive about photos, especially if taken by Americans, of what for them is a special place. But a few of us couldn't help ourselves, and we tried to discretely snap away. "No photography, no photography," a civilian on the street upbraided us. We stopped. Later, several of us went back to sneak in some more "photography" of the former American embassy.

Early on in our tour a young man mysteriously joined our group and went everywhere we went. He was way too inquisitive and intrusive. At one point he challenged Wally Shellenberger. Having discovered Wally has great respect for Islam, he wanted to know why he didn't just convert to Islam. And when we met with several Christian leaders in Tehran, he became quite engaged in the conversation and clearly put the Christians on guard, making them less transparent with us.

There was some difference of opinion in our group about who this young man was and why he had joined us. Some wondered whether he was a minder and would later report back to government what he had observed with out group. Wally Shellenberger didn't think so; Mr. Haghani told him he had asked this young man to travel with us for awhile. He felt sorry for him because he had no father and he needed some income. But Wally resolved that this young man, whoever he was, couldn't continue with us. After several blunt conversations with Mr. Haghani, the young man apparently got the point. He bid us farewell, and he went on his way.

Everywhere in Iran there are pictures of the Ayatollah Khomeini, who is revered by many Iranians for throwing off Western influence in the country.

4 Heading for the hills

Young Nassrin herself reflected the complexity of the Iranian people about whom she spoke. The day she joined our tour group, our mini-bus climbed the hilly northern part of Tehran to visit the spartan, two-bedroom apartment where the Ayatollah Khomeini lived after the Islamic Revolution. (Iranians refer to him as *Imam* Khomeini.) This stop was immediately followed by a visit to the opulent palace where the Shah of Iran had lived.

Seeing these contrasting domiciles back-to-back was one of the few times on our trip when I felt as though I was subjected to propaganda: *Khomeini good, the Shah very bad*. Let me be clear: if I had to choose between the two, I would much prefer living in the more simple domicile where Khomeini lived than the garish palace of the Shah where many of the walls and ceilings were lined with ornate glass and mirrors. But I would hope to not have to choose between either regime.

On the way to Khomeini's apartment, I was sitting next to Nassrin, who told me that going to see his apartment is a deeply spiritual experience for her. It became quite clear that she adores the man, even though she is too young to remember the Islamic Revolution, and that she had a quite different image of this man than I or most Americans have. To her Khomeini was a man committed to peace and justice, a very spiritual person who feared no one or no nation; he feared God alone, she said.

If Khomeini was so spiritual, I wanted to ask, how he could have demonized the United States and the West the way he did, or refused to release the embassy hostages when greatly pressured by numerous third parties around the world? And what about the atrocities that occurred on his watch after the Revolution—the "wasting" of people who seemed to threaten the legitimacy of the new government; the shutting down of the free press, universities, and theaters; the expunging of anything that reflected Western culture? But unlike my earlier encounter with the ambassador, I held my peace, since the night before we had been encouraged by our American leaders to look for the good things in Iranian culture, and to listen before criticizing. So I listened and pondered her words, and it occurred to me that we don't get to choose another culture's heroes, that to try to do so is just one more form of cultural imperialism.

Shirin Ebadi, the Iranian judge who was demoted from a judgeship to a clerical position after the Islamic Revolution and subsequently won the Nobel Peace prize in 2003 for her fight for human rights, has said that "Iranians are at heart hero worshippers. . . . [T]hey cling to the notion that one lofty, iconic figure can sweep through their lives, slay their enemies, and turn their world around. Perhaps other cultures also believe in heroes," Ebadi says, "but Iranians do so with a unique devotion. Not only do they fall in love with heroes, but they are in love with their love for them."[9]

I saw this hero worship at work with young Nassrin, yet it also occurred to me that for many Iranians Imam Khomeini is their Gandhi or Mandela, their liberator from a tyrant leader and from unwanted and unwarranted Western influence and control in their country. Given the image we Americans have of Khomeini, this might be tough to admit, yet it is a reality we dare not dismiss or ignore. It is simply a form of cultural imperialism for us to try to choose another nation's heroes for them.

Although I held my tongue with Nassrin, I later learned that one of my co-travelers asked Nassrin about whether the atrocities that went along with the Revolution are written about in their school textbooks. She admitted atrocities happened, though they're not addressed in the textbooks. But they're "out there," she said, and are being talked about. Nassrin also said that her own parents were young supporters of the Revolution at the time it took place, yet other members of her extended family opposed it.

There are losses with any gains, Nassrin said. And with that she seemed to rationalize the death squads that snuffed out people who dared to speak out against the excesses of the new regime. Yes, Nassrin was correct: her country and her people are complex. And she reflected that complexity herself. But I couldn't help think that our own government doesn't even begin to understand this complexity, perhaps because we want to believe what we want about them, whatever the reality.

Personnel at a Red Crescent Society rehabilitation hospital in Tehran proudly show off hydrotherapy machines bought from France using Mennonite Central Committee funds.

7 The little NGO that could

Mennonite Central Committee (MCC) has had continuous involvement with Iran through the Red Crescent Society, going back to 1990 when there was a severe earthquake in northwestern Iran. When there is a big natural disaster in Iran some American nongovernmental organizations (NGOs) like CARE and Relief International will offer assistance. But MCC is the only Western NGO that has had continuous involvement in Iran during this period.

The 1990 earthquake killed over 30,000 people. In 1991 MCC responded with medical supplies, working through the Iranian Red Crescent Society. MCC was also interested in offering longer-term reconstruction assistance, so it agreed to provide financial assistance toward the construction and equipping of village health clinics in fifteen of the communities hit by the earthquake's devastation. After the Persian Gulf War of 1991, more than a million Iraqis took refuge in Iran. In response, MCC placed an American doctor and social worker in a refugee camp for a number of months.

In 1998 MCC began a student exchange program with Imam Khomeini Education and Research Institute (IKERI) in Qom. Students from North America go there to study Islam and Persian language, and students come to Toronto for doctoral studies in religion. The host committee covers all exchange student housing, medical, and financial needs.[10]

The city of Qom, a center of Shi'ite learning, is the religious capital of Iran. Home to one of Shi'a's most sacred shrines, there are somewhere between 40 and 60 seminaries in Qom—locals don't even know the exact number—with some 100,000 students, about 30 percent of whom are women. The Ayatollah Khomeini came from there and it was from Qom the Islamic Revolution of 1979 was organized and supported. Being a very conservative city, the idea of IKERI, which is devoted to the study of other religions, is itself controversial in Qom. There are no churches there and no known Christians in the city besides MCC exchange students. Indeed, the students themselves are considered to be American spies by some. The ethos of Qom is reviled in much of the rest of Iran.[11]

Starting in 2002 MCC has also cosponsored consultations between Mennonite and Islamic scholars/theologians from Iran. One of these meetings held in Waterloo, Ontario, drew press attention because Iranians in Canada protested MCC's involvement with IKERI and protested the Iranian government.

These exchanges enhance learning to know and respect the other but also highlight differences between the groups. Awkward encounters are inevitable: In Canada, Islamic guests were taken to a Mennonite church where some of the young people were dressed immodestly in a way offensive to their Islamic guests. In Iran Mennonite scholars were taken to a celebration of the twenty-fifth anniversary of the Islamic Revolution, and they were seated in the grandstands between military attaches from countries who sell arms to Iran and the clerics who run the country, wedding political power with Islamic beliefs.[12] And the Hanges, the first American couple to study in Qom, report that a five-year-old son of one of their classmates came home from his daycare center marching around the room saying, "Death to America." It was a slogan he learned at the daycare, the same one their own daughter attended.[13]

Nevertheless, they personally experienced many instances of Iranian graciousness and hospitality. And one of the opportunities that fell into Roy's lap was to teach John Howard Yoder's *The Politics of Jesus* to a class of Muslim seminary students studying Christianity at IKERI.[14]

MCC's most controversial engagement with Iran has been the series of meetings already mentioned with President Ahmadinejad. All but one of these meetings were held in New York City when he was there to attend the opening meetings of the United Nations in the fall. One was held in Tehran. The last two meetings in New York, which I attended as an invited journalist, included representatives of other denominations (2007) and even other religions (2008) to directly engage the very controversial president in dialogue.

While MCC has been very direct with the president about his denial of the Holocaust and his comments about ending the state of Israel,[15] MCC has taken heat for even dignifying the man by having such face-to-face meetings. In fact, the last of these meetings attracted a protest rally outside the Manhattan hotel where the dinner meeting was held. Not only were the telephone lines at MCC headquarters hot with calls from irate protestors, many of whom were not MCC constituents; other Mennonite institutions were getting complaints from people inclined to demonize Ahmadinejad.

While some would revile MCC's efforts at relief, development, and peacebuilding in Iran, what they have been able to do on a relatively modest budget has been rather remarkable. Indeed, it has not been sufficiently heralded. We can only imagine how the relationship between the U.S. and Iran might be transformed if the U.S. State Department were to put similar efforts into building bridges between the two countries, rather than trying to marginalize and punish Iran for its human rights violations and efforts at developing nuclear fuel.

Because of the longstanding working relationship with the Iranian Red Crescent Society, it was natural that our tour's first official visit was to the RCS headquarters located in a towering office building in northern Tehran. We were warmly greeted there by the director general of international affairs, his deputy, and two program directors. Three of these four administrators were women, one of whom has a doctorate. This surprised us Westerners, since we assumed that Iranian women have second-class status.

The representatives of RCS thanked us for MCC's involvement in Iran. Our delegation presented them with a peace lamp made by Mennonite potter Dick Lehman, one of twenty we gave to our hosts during our two weeks in Iran. It was explained that similar peace lamps were burning in many Mennonite churches in North America during the recent Advent season, inviting prayers of peace between our countries. Each lamp we gave had a card attached with a verse from the Qur'an and the Bible, with the common theme of light.

We were then given a tour of the rehabilitation hospitality next door to the RCS headquarters. It is a hospital which has treated war victims, including many of the people who were injured and maimed in the protracted Iraq-Iran war in the 1980s. Many of their patients have had to be fitted with prosthesis. In one room remembering the war victims there was a copy of a computer printout that recorded the identities of all the people known to have been killed or injured in this war, a printout that must have been at least six inches thick—a stark reminder of the brutal hostility between Saddam Hussein and the Ayatollah Khomeini.

The personnel at the hospital quite proudly pointed out to us hydrotherapy machines that had been bought from France using MCC funds. One member of our group asked whether the U.S. sanctions against Iran made it difficult for them to obtain medical equipment. The doctor who served as our tour guide said no, that they are able to purchase what they need from other countries.

I was surprised to see several posters on the hospital walls in English. One pictured Grant Hill, African-American basketball star, when he still played for the Detroit Pistons. The other was an Iranian advertisement for tinted contact lens. Apparently the company name was Aryan, based on the fact that ethnically most Iranians are Aryan. And their company slogan was "For clear and beautiful eyes." I came to the conclusion after two weeks of taking pictures of Iranians that most of them didn't need to have tinted contact lens; even without them they had expressive eyes, and many had beautiful eyes—naturally!

When we walked out of the rehabilitation hospital we had a panoramic view of the city before us. But what caught my eye was a sign with a verse from the Qur'an which read, "Help one another in goodness and piety," a verse which seemed to me to resonate with my Mennonite sensibility about faith and works needing to go together. Then I began to notice the first of many "alms boxes" along the street. Diamond-shaped boxes mounted on parking-meter type posts, they appeared on at least every other block, a constant reminder to the people that "alms-giving" is an essential element in Islamic piety.

The shape of the dome on an Armenian Orthodox Church in the city of Esfahan mimics a mosque, but it has a discrete Christian cross at the top.

8 Human rights and wrongs

A constant source of conversation within our American delegation was the issue of human rights violations in Iran and how hard we should push our Iranian interlocutors about this. Several young adults in our group said we were giving a pass to the Iranian leaders we talked with, that we needed to be more upfront with them about human rights issues in relation to women and religious minorities in particular. Others in our group with significant international experience, including with authoritarian governments like Iran's, said that we needed to go slowly, that we were going to be in the country only two weeks, and that we were their guests and must be cautious about calling them to accountability over human rights issues.

In conversations with government leaders in Tehran, university professors in Shiraz, and Islamic clerics in Qom, we Americans were quick to confess the sins of our government, yet the Iranians rarely said anything negative about their own. To be sure, this reflects a cultural difference. But they have much more at stake if they speak out, especially among peers, against their own government. Indeed, a recent Human Rights Watch report on Iran says that the number of people imprisoned on vague charges continues to increase. Iranians with foreign contacts are particularly vulnerable to government suppression.

Despite their understandable reticence to speak up in group settings, when we got some of our Iranian hosts alone they were more open to admit in a general way that there are problems. One older professor said that leading up to the Islamic Revolution his students were religious activists protesting against the Shah. Now many of his students are mildly opposing the current regime's use of religion, with less than hopeful results. He didn't go into detail, and we didn't press him.

When we visited Archbishop Sarkissian of the Armenian Orthodox Church in Iran, he told us that whether groups in Iran have religious freedom depends on what is meant by freedom. It also depends on which group you're talking about. The Armenian Orthodox Church doesn't pose much of a threat to the government because they are a "national church." One must be born into their church, in other words, and by nature the Orthodox do not evangelize or proselytize. Still, the Armenian Orthodox are losing their people to emigration. While there are still about 100,000 of them, each year 2-3,000 emigrate elsewhere, thanks in part to the intervention of the Hebrew Immigrant Aid Society, a Zionist organization that is also encouraging Christians to leave the country. The archbishop said this group is decimating his people and asked us to go back to the U.S. and speak out against them.

There is a section of the city of Esfahan called New Joffa, where the Armenians live. New Joffa, of course, is named after the city of Joffa in Armenia where their ancestors came from. We visited the Orthodox church in New Joffa, which has a striking profile: the dome, though plain colored, is shaped like the domes on Muslim mosques. Yet very discretely, at the apex of the dome, is a small cross. Beside the church there is a museum dedicated to remembering the Armenian genocide that took place in Turkey. I asked an Armenian student visiting the church and museum what life is like for him in Iran as a non-Muslim. He responded, "That's a dangerous question." I didn't press it.

Oddly enough, the courtyard of this church and museum was decorated for Christmas. There was even a fake Santa Claus as part of the display, and Christmas music was being played

over a sound system. Much of it was secular American Christmas music. Before we left, a live Santa Claus arrived. Evie told
us that the Christians here send a confusing message to the
Muslims in Iran. The Muslims want to know where Santa
Claus is talked about in the Bible.

The human rights situation is even more difficult for the
Armenian Evangelical Church, which is really Presbyterian, but
they don't use that word because it is associated with the West.
They have one central church in Tehran, plus two house
churches. Their pastor left the country for the United States,
and his predecessor was killed in the 1990s, apparently because
he was too critical of the government. One leader from this
group told us that their church's biggest challenge is to maintain
a sense of hope. When I asked her what gives her hope for the
future, there was a long pause. Then she said she was probably
the wrong person to ask. We later found out that this pastor was
planning to emigrate to the United States to join a community
of Amenian evangelicals in southern California, including the
former pastor of their church in Tehran.

We heard reports too that things are much more difficult
for Farsi-speaking Christian churches, especially the more
evangelical or Pentecostal groups that try to evangelize. Unfortunately, we didn't get a chance to talk with any of these groups.

The Jewish community too is under duress. One Friday afternoon, before Shabbat services, we visited a synagogue in Esfahan. Ironically, it is located on Palestinian Square, across from
a mosque and a bank, just down from a Christian church. Evidence of Jewish presence in Esfahan goes back 2,500 years. A
lay leader there told us that at one time there were twenty-five
synagogues in the city; now they're down to ten. Although he
predicted 300 people would attend Shabbat services that
evening, there are no more rabbis left in the country. Once in
awhile they get a visiting rabbi from Israel or the U.S., but synagogue leadership is totally in the hands of the laity.

Iranians are understandably reticent to criticize their government, unlike we Americans, who can speak out with im-

punity against what we don't like coming out of Washington. But Iranians must fear imprisonment—or worse—for being critical of the powers that be.

I did have two encounters, however, in which individuals were quick to voice dislike of the mullahs who run the country. The first was on a Friday afternoon, Islam's holy day, when we visited a park-like setting beside the Zayandeh River by the Si-o-Seh Bridge, an architectural beauty with thirty-three arches. Much of the time when we were in Iran it was atypically cold and snowy. But on this Friday afternoon it was relatively warm and sunny. And it brought out the people, hundreds of people.

A large crowd had gathered around some men who were singing traditional Iranian folks songs. They were sung by solo voices without accompaniment. After each song, the crowd vigorously gave their approval with clapping. Our Esfahan guide later told us that the singer who received the most attention is a famous TV personality.

Almost immediately after I got off the bus and started to explore the park-like setting by the bridge, I was approached by a man who spoke very good English. Now retired, he had been a pilot in the military before the fall of the Shah. Twice he had gone to the United States for training on military bases. He made it very clear that he likes the United States, and he spoke nostalgically of his training time in the U.S.

He applauded President Bush for going after the Taliban in Afghanistan, although with some justification he accused the U.S. of helping to create the Taliban in the first place to fight the 1980s Soviet occupation of Afghanistan. While he had no tolerance for Saddam Hussein, he thought it a mistake for the United States to topple him. Without Saddam to hold Iran in check, he feared that the radical Islamicists running his own country were now too emboldened and up to no good. He even referred to the mullahs running Iran as "soft Taliban."

The other occasion when an Iranian was openly critical of the Iranian government came at the beginning of our second week in Iran. First some background.

The first week we had slowly made our way by minibus from Tehran in the north (up near the Caspian Sea) down through the cities of Qom, Kashan, Esfahan, and Shiraz (down toward the Persian Gulf). To save time, we then were to fly back to Tehran the following Monday evening and drive back to the city of Qom where we were to stay for the rest of the week to hear lectures from professors at the Imam Khomeini Education and Research Institute (IKERI). By the time we were to leave Shiraz it had gotten very cold and snowy. When we got to the airport late afternoon, all the flights were canceled, except for ours, which was to leave early evening. But it kept getting postponed.

At last, around midnight, we were told we could board our plane, which meant walking out onto the tarmac and climbing up a mobile stairs into the plane. While walking out we noticed that some men were actually shoveling show off the runway with hand shovels. After another delay, sitting on the plane, we were told we would have to move to another plane, which we again did on foot. And that plane was having a tire changed while the plane itself seemed to be jacked up with a car jack.

Finally we took off around 1:30 a.m. and got into Tehran around 3 a.m. Instead of driving to Qom yet that night, we went back to the hotel we had stayed at the first few nights in Tehran, just around the corner from the former U.S. Embassy. We all fell into bed and tried to get as much sleep as we could.

The next morning, in the hotel lobby, we had a chance meeting with four very friendly seamen. The talkative one told us that since 9-11 they're restricted in where they can go. They can't port in the United States. Years ago, when they ported in Canada, they were free to roam around. Now their movements are restricted and they're greeted in Canadian ports by soldiers with guns. Once, when in Australia, they were asked if they were terrorists!

The spokesmen of this group said that when he gets around the world, he sees that other people have it so much better than Iranians do. Despite the fact he has four children, sometimes he tells his wife that he may not come home again, that he'll settle elsewhere. He has no time at all for his own government. They concern themselves with foreign affairs and do nothing about their domestic problems like high unemployment, especially among the young people. It only makes matters worse when they do things in the name of God. Politics that uses religion ends up corrupting religion, he asserted.

The seaman said he thought the U.S. did the right thing going into Afghanistan, taking out the Taliban. But it was a huge mistake to invade Iraq. Besides the loss of life there, including many women and children, it has only made his own country a stronger, and therefore more menacing, presence in the Middle East. Remarkably, he still thought the U.S. had a stabilizing influence in the Middle East.

How should we weigh the significance of these critical voices? In that both of these examples came from persons with great admiration for the U.S., I would have to say they represent a minority, especially their pro-Americanism. Yet I suspect the criticism that their own government attempts to throw its weight around internationally while neglecting economic realities on the home front speaks for many Iranians.

A more nuanced perspective came from some business professor we met. They were particularly interested in asking us questions about the presidential primaries in the United States, even asking specific questions about the Iowa caucus, which Barack Obama had just won on the Democratic side. What seemed to interest them most was the interplay between religion and politics in the United States. So they wondered about the influence of evangelicals in the electoral process. And they wanted to know more about Mitt Romney, who was then running for president in the Republican primary, and his Mormon religion. The questions seemed to suggest that Romney was being discriminated against on account of his Mormonism.

One professor, an economist who had studied in the United States, asked most of the questions. He had done his doctorate at the University of Pennsylvania. This professor admitted to us that it is very difficult to be open in Iran about any dissent from the government. He was already teaching at the time of the Islamic Revolution, and then his students were pushing back against the tyranny of the Shah. In fact, the student resistance was largely motivated by religion. Now there is a student reaction against the religious rule of Iran, but it is not meeting with good results.

In this setting, once again we Americans were freely critical about the sins of our own government. The professors didn't reciprocate. I had to wonder, though, how much more the American-trained economist would have said to us privately if he hadn't had to worry about any repercussions.

All women, including international visitors, are expected to wear the hijab *(head covering) in public. The women using pay phones most likely are voluntarily wearing the* chador *(a large piece of cloth, usually black) over top of the hijab.*

9 Head coverings

Another source of conversation within our American group was the mandatory wearing of the hijab (head covering) by women. The women in our tour group had been advised ahead of time that they needed to wear a headscarf covering their hair, and a loose-fitting coat that came down to at least the knees. While each was prepared for this, most weren't prepared for their emotional reaction to always needing to wear this garb in public. The women shared in our group meetings that while wearing this garb made them feel safer, it also made them feel like second-class citizens. One woman said that she found the hijab psychologically toxic. "It makes me feel invisible in groups," she said, and "less free to speak up." She called it a cage in which she felt trapped.

The women in our group also pointed out to us men that the Iranian women tended not to talk or at least to take a back seat to Iranian men in mixed-group settings. In response, we American men encouraged the American women to speak up more, and we men pledged not to dominate discussions with Iranians.

On two separate occasions the wearing of the hijab came up in lectures that were given on our behalf at the Imam Khomeni Education and Research Institute, where we spent four days. Our lecturers in Qom were all men, of course—clerics—and several tried explaining to us the importance of women wearing the hijab in Islamic culture. *Hijab* really means the covering of the hair and the body. It is necessary, said one professor, because men are more attracted to women than women to men, and because women enjoy being looked at. It is for the benefit of the woman, as when she is covered she is less likely to be misused. But it is also for the benefit of the society and the family, since sexual desire should be limited to the family.

Where the hijab isn't observed, the satisfaction of sexual desire becomes of greater interest in that society. When women are not covered outside the home it is like opening a perfume bottle for all to consume, whereas the "perfume" should be restricted to the family. Society has a right to make some rules for the benefit of the whole society, he said, like the mandatory wearing of seat belts, even if not everyone agrees that seat belts—or the hijab—should be worn.

There is a very funny video on YouTube by an Islamic humorist, with a serious point. When Catholic nuns wear the habit, he says, Christians say she's practicing her religion. But when Muslim women wear it, it is said she's oppressed. Okay, there's a double standard there. It is clear that many Muslim women voluntarily wear the hijab as a sincere expression of their religious devotion. Yet in a place like Iran women have no choice, whether Muslim or not, whether observant or not. One of our delegates diplomatically pointed out to a lecturer that in France young Muslim girls are forbidden to wear the hijab to public school; in Iran all women must wear it regardless, whereas in the U.S. Muslim girls and women have the freedom to wear it if they wish. Which approach is better?

One young Iranian mother told us that her five-year-old daughter is already asking her why females in Iran must wear a headscarf. What am I to tell her? she asked us. She said that children and youth in Iran are exposed to the wider world through the Internet and the satellite dish, which will most certainly lead to cultural changes in the future, which of course is what some of the clerics are worried about. Here's another thing for them to worry about: Almost the moment our plane left the ground in Tehran, enroute back to Frankfurt, most of the hijabs came off the women, including the Iranian women.

After we visited the Armenian Orthodox church in Tehran, the one woman in our group shared with us what she had experienced there. The first thing she saw in the archbishop's office was a picture of Jesus, she said. She's not ordinarily moved by pictures of Jesus, but to her surprise this time she was. And then the archbishop told our women that they were in a Christian place and they didn't have to wear the hijab. When she took off the hijab at his invitation, she experienced all over again what it means to be free in Christ.

Iran is home to many refugees, including this Afghan shepherd who was eager to interact with our tour group.

10 Welcoming the stranger?

On Wednesday of our first week in Iran we traveled from the town of Kashan to the ancient city of Esfahan. According to one legend, Kashan is the place from which the wise men started to follow the star to the place of Jesus' birth. It's just a legend, understand; who can know? Esfahan is a very ancient and beautiful city, with two of the most exquisite mosques of any place in the world—the "blue" mosque and the "women's" mosque. These mosques are connected to a huge mall and a four-kilometer-long, indoor bazaar where it is easy to get lost.

In Iran it is not only mosque and state that are connected; there is a cozy relationship between mosque, state, and the bazaar. In fact, bazaar owners were some of the most ardent supporters of the Islamic Revolution and to this day remain big supporters of Iran leaders.

To get to Esfahan our mini-bus had to climb over a rugged mountain range. On one ascent the bus started to make a funny noise. It was no surprise to me: From the moment we left our Tehran hotel on the first day in Iran, I had thought the bus didn't sound very good, and I wondered how reliable it would be. Besides, it gave off noxious fumes that filtered into the bus and at first made me feel ill. After several days I got used to it.

I'm not mechanical at all yet have an uncanny sense when something doesn't sound right mechanically. While the engine seemed to be giving up the ghost, our driver coaxed it on a half mile or so, then it died, and he pulled it to the side of the modern, four-lane highway on which we were traveling. The driver tried repeatedly to get the engine going again, but like a stubborn mule it wasn't cooperating. Our option seemed clear: We would have to call a backup van so that we could proceed on our way. In what seemed like the middle of nowhere, remarkably Mr. Haghani's cell phone worked. Thankfully.

Some of us had noticed a shepherd with a flock of sheep and goats back down the hill. So when we piled out of the bus to stretch our legs, some of us agreed that we would walk back down the highway and observe the shepherd and his flock. It was like a scene out of Matthew 25, where Jesus talked about separating the sheep from the goats and doing good to "the least of these": feeding the hungry, giving drink to the thirsty, welcoming the stranger, clothing the naked, taking care of the sick, and visiting the imprisoned.

As we stood by the side of the road, watching the shepherd and his sheep dogs moving the flock on the side of the hill, we attracted his attention. Through David Wolfe and Linda Kusse-Wolfe, a Quaker couple who had joined our group, we were able to communicate with him a bit. (They were then part of the MCC student-exchange program in Qom.) The shepherd, we discovered, was an Afghan refugee. This job in central Iran was the only one he could find. His whole family was still back in Afghanistan, and he indicated things were not good for them there. He was pleased that we wanted to take his picture. In fact, one of our group members had a Polaroid camera with him for the sake of taking pictures of people we met and giving them a copy. When the shepherd saw his picture slowing forming on the print, he asked for another picture to be taken of himself so that he could send it back to his family.

The Afghan shepherd cast a compelling visage: white beard, ruddy complexion, bright eyes that nearly danced, and an engaging smile. The young women and the old men in Iran seemed the most photogenic Iranians. Usually you couldn't seem anything more than the women's faces, but what faces they were! Their skin was radiant, their eyes dark, yet brilliant, and they often would great us with warm smiles. What was compelling about the old men was the ruggedness of their faces and their white beards that would contrast with their olive-toned complexion.

The Afghan shepherd was particularly drawn to James Cooper's beard. Beards are highly regarded in Afghanistan, the longer the better. The shepherd stroked and even kissed James' beard, and James was a good sport about it all.

As part of the orientation for our trip we were encouraged ahead of time to bring small gifts with us to give to the people we met and our various hosts. Before leaving home I had gone to Trader Joe's and picked up some chocolate bars for this purpose. Thankfully, I had one bar in my coat pocket. I pulled it out and gave it to the Afghan shepherd, and his eyes lit up like stars. I imagined that his life in these remote hills must be very difficult, and that he seldom if ever had a treat like chocolate or other simple pleasures. I imagined him savoring this candy bar later than night, perhaps just eating a little bit at a time to make it stretch as long as possible.

Before we returned to our bus—a newer, more reliable bus picked us up eventually—Linda Kusse-Wolfe told the shepherd she'd be praying for him and his family. He seemed pleased by that gesture too.

What I didn't know before going to Iran is that the country has been a host to thousands—millions, actually—of immigrants like this Afghan. According to the UNHCR, 950,000 refugees in Iran were officially registered in 2007, but the actual number is considerably higher than that—as many as two million. Most of them are, like the shepherd, from Afghanistan.

There are also refugees from Iraq, both Iraqi Shiites and Kurds, many of whom came during the Iran-Iraq War (1980-88). Most of the Kurds have since been repatriated, but about 200,000 ethnic Iranians from Iraq have been permanently settled in Iran. The Afghans started arriving in 1980. They often live in squalid conditions, and they occupy the lowest rung on the social ladder. They take on menial jobs, and they don't have full access to education and health care like Iranian citizens do. They are often treated very shabbily, and since the fall of the Taliban in Afghanistan, Iran has been trying to encourage the immigrants to return home.[16]

One evening in the second week of our trip, we met with a group of Muslim seminarians in the city of Qom. These students have been part of a cross-cultural and educational exchange started by Dan Wessner, then of Eastern Mennonite University, a member of our tour group. These students from Iran and other students around the world—including several universities in the United States and one in Vietnam—watch the same movies periodically throughout the year. Then they blog about what they saw in the movies and students get a first-hand experience of seeing how people from other cultures respond to the same cinema. Movies are chosen from all over the world, including Iranian ones. The most difficult country from which to choose movies that are acceptable are those from the United States, since they have too much gratuitous sex and violence, an offense to the Iranians.

The evening we met with the seminary students in Qom we viewed together an Iranian film, *Baran*. The setting is a construction site that uses illegal aliens from Afghanistan for cheap labor and treats them as less than full human beings. After the viewing, we sat in a circle and discussed the film. I mentioned in the discussion that I couldn't help but think of how poorly Mexican immigrants are treated in the United States.

One of the Iranian seminarians responded that he thought that Mexican immigrants are treated much more poorly in our country than Afghan immigrants in Iran. There was nothing to be gained by arguing the point over who mistreats immigrants the most, especially illegal ones. But the stated perception was nevertheless interesting—our immigrants must surely have it worse than theirs! Obviously, we both have an immigrant problem—a fear of the "other," a marginalizing and oppression of people different from ourselves, people who are merely trying to make a decent living for the family.

This statue remains among the ruins at Persepolis, a massive palace conceived by King Darius in 518 BC, which was considered one of the greatest architectural achievements of its time.

11 Under the surface

Iranian culture is like a tapestry, with different elements existing side by side. Some people in the culture identify with some parts of the tapestry more than others. And clashes in the culture come from parts of this tapestry rubbing against each other.

One dominant aspect of this tapestry since the Islamic Revolution is the strict, stern Shi'a religion imposed on the people by the mullahs who run the country. Another part of the Iranian tapestry is the ancient Persian culture that preceded the Islamic Republic of Iran by 2,500 years.

The most important holiday in Iran is Nowruz, the New Year's celebration, that takes place around the spring equinox and lasts for thirteen days. Everything shuts down for lots of eating, dancing, reciting of poetry, and building of fires that dance back and forth. It's not an Islamic celebration: rather, it's a holdover from Zoroastrianism, Persia's traditional religion. At times some clerics have tried to disband the New Year celebrations or replace it with another holiday. However, one Iranian says, "They couldn't get rid of Nowruz because we've been practicing Nowruz for 2,500 years. They don't really control us, because they can't control what's inside."[17]

One of Iran's most valued treasures is Persepolis, which we visited on our way to the city of Shiraz. Persepolis was once a massive palace sitting fifty feet above the ground, which originally took the space of nearly five football fields. The brainchild of King Darius in 518 BC, it was considered one of the greatest architectural achievements of its time. It was used for a spring festival celebrated by Zoroastrianism, the native religion of Persia. Unfortunately, Alexander the Great set the place on fire in 331 BC, destroying much of it, and invading Arabs defiled some of what was left in the seventh century AD and foreign archaeologists stole some of what remained in the nineteenth and twentieth centuries. Only a few of the 550 columns still remain, yet there is enough left of the statuary and artwork to get a sense of the grandeur it once had.

In the city of Shiraz in southern Iran we saw evidence of a later period of Persian culture when we visited the tombs and shrines of Sa'di and Hafez, two of Iran's most revered poets who lived in the thirteenth and fourteenth centuries respectively. The poetry of both these revered poets represents a blending of both Persian culture and Islamic religion. (Both were Sunnis, it should be pointed out.)

Iran has war memorials, to be sure, but what does it say about a country that reveres its poets and their burial sites are popular tourist attractions? Sa'di's tomb is inside an open stone colonnade which supports a beautiful tiled dome. Inside the dome there are inscriptions of famous lines from his poetry. Iranians are particularly proud that a verse from Sa'di is inscribed above the entrance to the United Nations building in New York City.

> Human beings are members of a whole,
> In creation of one essence and soul.
> If one member is afflicted with pain,
> Other members uneasy will remain.
> If you have no sympathy for human pain,
> The name of human you cannot retain.

The guide we had while in Shiraz told us that Sa'di, who was born in Shiraz, went to a university in Baghdad. After he graduated, he traveled for about thirty years through many countries in the Middle East, and then he came back home, where he wrote four books and lived another thirty years.

Hafez' marble tombstone is inside a shrine over which an octagonal pavilion was built with a tiled dome. Here too there is an engraving of a long verse by Hafez. Everyone in Iran, well educated or not, is able to quote some lines from Hafez, which function somewhat like biblical proverbs. There is also a practice of having one's future foretold by randomly opening to a page of his writings and letting an interpretation of that page serve as a predictor of the future.

When we visited Hafez' tomb we bumped into an Iranian family now living in Harrisburg, Pennsylvania. The three of them—a mother, father, and university-aged daughter, were back home in Iran for a visit. The daughter, who is studying biology and women's studies at Penn State University, told us that Americans tend to get caught up in appearances when we should be looking beneath the surface. Don't be hung up by women having to wear the hijab, she told us, but be concerned about human rights of women, such as divorce laws which give the advantage to men. When I asked her what it is like to be back home in Iran, she said it is much more relaxing in Iran than in the United States. And as much as things change in Iran, the scents remain the same.

The father was more outspoken. He doesn't trust the media in the United States, and the Israeli lobby has too much power. The U.S. media play up the worst rhetoric of President Ahmadinejad, whereas they ignored his predecessor, President Khatami who was open to a conversation with the West. He doesn't like Ahmadinejad, either, whom he referred to as an inexperienced politician and a "kid," a putdown I had heard before. U.S. backing of the Shah for nearly thirty years destroyed many of the social institutions in Iran, with the exception of the mosques. The mosques moved into the vacuum, which helped precipitate the Islamic Revolution in Iran.

Late in the afternoon of the same day we visited the tombs of the revered poets, we were the honored guest of the Ayatollah

Ha'eri Shirazi, the regional representative of the Supreme Leader of Iran, Khamenei. Our group was ushered into a room where there were a number of TV cameras and lights, as well as still photographers scurrying about. We were invited to sit in the front rows, right by the table where the ayatollah would eventually sit down. I was directly in his line of sight, only a few feet away from him, when he began to talk.

The previous MCC learning tour had not had a very good experience visiting the ayatollah in Shiraz. He had taken the occasion to attack the Mennonites for not being willing to fight—literally—for the oppressed. One should be willing to kill ten people to save one million, he had told them. With our group he took another approach. Indeed he preached at us, and I was turned off by much of what he had to say at the beginning, which was largely a platonic view of the human being. "When I look into the mirror," he said, "I see myself. But that is not really me. The real me is the spiritual self in relationship with God." While such a view is not uncommon, it struck me as being so foreign to what we Christians confess, at least at our best. We are a unified self of mind, body, and spirit into whom God breathes the breath of life. The incarnation is an indication that God honors the body, the material, and doesn't see it as inferior to the spiritual.

The ayatollah went on to talk about the relationship between Islam and Christianity. The Qur'an, he pointed out to us, instructs Muslims to read the Old and New Testaments. If you believe in the Qur'an, you also believe in the Bible. Further, Muslims also believe in Jesus, who is one in a line of prophets including Abraham, Moses, and, of course, Muhammed. "We cannot separate God from Jesus. If I reject Jesus, I have rejected God," he said. "He who follows Muhammed follows Jesus." All Abrahamic faiths are branches of a single tree, he claimed.

Then the ayatollah talked about peace. He had clearly adopted a different approach from the encounter with the last group of Mennonites who had visited him. "I congratulate you in your holy work of peace," he told us. "You are prophets because you are trying for peace. Jesus said that his true followers are those who work for peace. You are true Christians, and all true Christians are honored in Islam. There is no place for war in the divine kingdom," he said. "True followers of God will try for peace. Those who pursue war will go to hell, while those who seek peace will reach paradise."

No one in our group knew why the ayatollah took a different stance in relating to us compared to the previous Mennonite group. In any case, most of our group was taken in by the ayatollah. But I remained unmoved, as it still seemed to me that he was preaching at us, that he didn't really want to engage us. And his view of material reality, including the body, as being inferior to spiritual reality, had turned me off from the start.

And then in debriefing the sermon, which lasted an hour, some members of our group were willing to give up the Trinity in the interest of interfaith relations with Muslims, who are very strict monotheists. I'm very uncomfortable going that route. It seems to me basic to the Christian faith to acknowledge that when we say God we are talking about the one God who is nevertheless triune in nature—the God who creates, redeems and sanctifies us, the God whom we call Father, Son, and Holy Spirit.

Still, the ayatollah was trying to project a different image this time around: The next day our bus was summoned back to his headquarters. And he had a personal gift for each one of us—a desk pen and holder set.

The media coverage of our meeting with the ayatollah astounded us. But it likely said more about the importance of the ayatollah in the political scheme of things in Shiraz than about how important we were as his foreign guests. Mr. Haghani, our Iranian tour guide, said he saw our group meeting with the ayatollah on the news that evening. And the next night, when we flew out of Shiraz late at night—in the middle of a snow storm—all the seats on the plane had local newspapers. And there we were, pictures of our group meeting with the ayatollah.

Our tour group was graciously hosted for a meal in the home of Professor Legenhausen. Legenhausen, raised in a German Catholic home in the United States, now teaches Western philosophy in the holy city of Qom.

12 An American in Iran

Even before we left for Iran, our American leaders had told us that Dr. Muhammad Legenhausen would be one of our major resource persons in Iran. Our leaders had forwarded to us an email message from Dr. Legenhausen in which he had encouraged us to think of our trip to Iran as a spiritual pilgrimage. That sentiment resonated with me, since I had already decided that I didn't need to take God to Iran, that God is already there, and that my task was going to be to try to see where God is present in Iran. Dr. Legenhausen gave us some advance travel advice, drawing from Islam. "The friend, then the road," Dr. Legenhausen quoted from the Great Prophet, meaning that before one travels one should find some good traveling companions.

Legenhausen, I had thought to myself: that sounds German, not Persian. And I was correct about his ethnic background but not his national origin. As it turned out, he had grown up in Queens, New York, in a Catholic family. He had gone to Catholic parochial schools, but by college he had rejected the Catholic faith, in part because he thought his church should have taken a clear stance against the Vietnam War. He and only one other student in his Catholic elementary school opposed the war. Already in high school he had shown signs of his future career teaching philosophy, since he had taken an interest in Søren Kierkegaard.

After some graduate education, Legenhausen took a job teaching at Texas Southern University. The college where he was teaching was deliberately recruiting foreign students, and among them were some Muslim students whose religious discipline and devotion impressed Legenhausen and piqued his curiosity. So on his own he started studying Islam and found himself drawn to it, first as an academic subject but then eventually as a personal pursuit.

Like an evangelical who can tell you precisely when he experienced his own conversion, Legenhausen can identify the time when he converted to Islam. Some African-American students asked him when he had become Muslim, and he spontaneously responded with the central "creed" of Islam, "There is no god but Allah, and Muhammad is his Prophet." And then he began to weep. The students asked him to serve as faculty sponsor for a Muslim group and he started arranging for prayers at the university.

Eventually Legenhausen got a doctorate in philosophy and was invited to a visiting lectureship in Tehran for a year. Then he was asked to teach Western and comparative philosophy at the Imam Khomeini Education and Research Institute in Qom, where he is to this day. Through a friend he met his future wife, a bright Iranian woman who allows Westerners to call her Heidi. They have a bright-eyed and studious thirteen-year-old son Ali, who is painfully shy but quite devoted to his father.

Legenhausen told us that the West does not really know Shi'a Islam, which is by far the dominant Muslim group in Iran. That may partly explain why President Bush was famously quoted in the early years of the Iraq war, "I thought they were just all Muslims," when briefed about the differences between Sunni and Shi'a Muslims. This is like making no distinctions between Catholic, Protestant, or Orthodox Christians. Legenhausen said that all the Western textbooks introduce Islam through the Sunni perspective, because Western Orientalists first learned Islam from the Ottoman Empire, which was Sunni, and later from Egypt, which is also Sunni.

Westerners are taught, for instance, about the Five Pillars of Islam: the Oneness of God and the finality of the prophethood of Muhammad, saying of the daily prayers, almsgiving to the needy, fasting during Ramadan (called Ramazan in Iran), and (at least) once-in-a-lifetime pilgrimage to Mecca for those who are able. While these convictions are integral to Shi'a Islam, the Shi'a don't use this kind of "pillar" language. What distinguishes the Shi'a is who they accept as the legitimate successors to Muhammad and what role they play in Islam. (For more on this Shi'a distinction, see Tom Finger, p. 110 ff.)

The Shi'a have the same five prayers as Sunnis, but differences in the ways the Shi'a interpret Islamic law allow the Shi'a to combine the timings of some of the prayers so that there are three times a day in which they pray. The Shi'a perform the afternoon prayers right after the noon prayers and the evening prayers right after the sunset prayers, making three prayers a day instead of five. Sunnis and Shi'a also have different understandings about the justice of God: Sunnis believe that God can make laws arbitrarily, Shi'a do not. That would go against reason, they say. This results in Shi'a being more concerned about justice on a human plane, too.

Legenhausen said that saying prayers in the mosque is not as important to Shi'as as Sunnis. He rarely goes to mosque himself, yet he prays three times a day—in his office or home, wherever he is. Many devout Muslims belong to what he called religious societies that are organized around a common cause: it may be to read and study the Qur'an together or to participate in some kind of social service. Some of these religious societies invite clerics to preach for them, and some of them have their own buildings.

Muslims believe that all the great prophets had a book revealed to them, and that the Gospels were revealed to the Prophet Jesus. Legenhausen acknowledged that this is anachronistic: The Gospels came after Jesus, not from Jesus. Yet Legenhausen has worked on an interesting thesis that maintains the truth of the Qur'an and the New Testament: that it was the gospel itself that was revealed to Jesus as reflected in both his life and teachings.

In Iran, the line between religion and politics is blurred. One example is that on Friday, their holy day, two sermons are given in all the mosques throughout the country. One of the two sermons should be about the rules of Islam and the other about current political affairs. The Friday prayer leaders are appointed by the supreme leader, but they compose their own sermons.

Legenhausen also agreed with Nassrin that Iran is a complex country. Although he hasn't given up his American citizenship, he has lived in Iran now for two decades yet still doesn't understand the political system. One assumption many have in the West is that the supreme leader is a dictator and the president his instrument, Legenhausen told us. But in reality, power is not as concentrated with the few as many think.

Bush's "axis of evil" speech baffled most Iranians, according to Legenhausen. It not only came after 9-11, when the Iranians had been helpful to the United States in battling the Taliban in Afghanistan; it also came when President Khatami was president of the country. Khatami was a reform-minded leader who was more open to the West, advocating a "dialogue among civilizations" rather than a clash between them. He tried to improve human rights within Iran itself, especially for women. But when Bush lumped Iran with Iraq and North Korea as part of the axis of evil, the response of some Iranians was to say, "If this is what we get from the U.S. when we have a reform-minded president, then perhaps what we need is a more aggressive kind of nationalistic leader." And they voted in the radical Ahmadinejad at the next election.

The "axis of evil," of course, alludes to the "Axis powers" during World War II—the coalition of dictator-led countries: Germany, Italy, and Japan. But there is no real coalition between Iran, Iran, and North Korea. Iraq is Iran's mortal enemy. How could they be lumped together? Besides, there is a deep and abiding rift between Iranians, who are Persians, and the

Arab world, including Iraq. And then to be lumped in with North Korea, led by the seemingly unstable Kim Jong-il, was of course an offense to the Iranians. No matter how bad Iran's leaders are, they are at least not starving their people.

Moreover, thoughtful Iranians think the U.S. and their allies speak out of both sides of their mouths. When the reform-minded Khatami was president, Western leaders said that he wasn't the real power in Iran; the real power—head of state and commander in chief—was the supreme leader. But when the belligerent Ahmadinejad came into power, Western countries treated him as though he were the one with the ultimate power. What gives here? Iranians wonder. The West seems to want to have it both ways, depending on what is in its perceived interest.

Legenhausen speculated that if the United States continues to try to call the shots in the Gulf region and the rest of the Middle East, Iran will most likely continue to be a pain in the neck. Iran just won't go along with the American program.

*The opulent palace of the Shah of Iran stands in the hilly ter-
rain of northern Tehran. The U.S. put the Shah in power after
toppling the democratically elected government of President
Mossadeq in 1953.*

13 What we don't know

There are some inconvenient truths about the relationship of the U.S. and Iran that many Americans don't know and others would like to ignore. First among them is the fact that in 1953 a CIA-sponsored coup brought down the government of Prime Minister Mossadeq, who was the democratically elected leader of the country at the time.

Mossadeq's crime was to nationalize Iran's greatest natural resource—petroleum—in response to foreign oil companies who were taking advantage of Iran's national treasure. A British oil consortium—which later became British Petroleum (BP)—had the most to lose from nationalization of Iranian oil. Iranians at first had hoped that the U.S. would come to their support in their struggle against the British. But instead, the U.S. actually did the dirty work for the Brits and in turn helped put the Shah of Iran back into power.

For twenty-five years thereafter the U.S. supported the Shah, who ruled brutally, suppressing or killing his opponents. Indeed, his notorious secret police, SAVAK, was financed and most likely trained by the U.S. But in politics as in physics, every action has an equal and opposite reaction. The reaction to the American support for the Shah was the formation of a loose coalition of very different and unlikely allies.

On one side were religious radicals who were opposed to any Western influence, in part on religious and cultural grounds—but also for the West's support of Israel and supposed opposition to Islam. Their inspiration came from the Ayatollah Khomeini, who because of his opposition to the Shah lived in exile from 1964-1979. The clerics who opposed the Shah were in large measure also backed by the merchants who had shops in the Bazaars throughout Iran, in part because the Shah's economic policies were detrimental to them.

The other part of the resistance to the American-backed shah came from leftists, Marxist intellectuals, and students. During the Cold War, the mere presence of Marxists in Iran gave the U.S. reason for supporting the Shah against his opposition.

The resistance to the Shah reached a crescendo in 1978. In response to some anti-Shah rallies in 1978, the Shah's henchmen killed many of the protesters. Right after one of these incidents, President Carter showed up in Tehran for a state dinner with the Shah. Carter deserves some credit for pressing the Shah to improve human rights in Iran, but after his meeting with the Shah, Carter publicly reaffirmed American support for the Shah. For some opponents of the Shah, this was the straw that broke the camel's back, leading to the demise and exile of the Shah, the return to Iran by the Ayatollah, the taking of hostages at the American embassy in Tehran, and the Islamic Revolution itself. The hostage-taking incident probably made Carter a one-term president.

Americans also conveniently forget that the U.S. supported Saddam Hussein in Iraq's eight-year with Iran. Sensing an opportunity to take advantage of Iran during a time of flux, Iraq invaded Iran in 1980. Thanks to U.S. support for Saddam, Iraq had superior weaponry, despite the fact the Reagan administration clandestinely sold some missiles to Iran through what became known as the Iran-Contra affair. Though deficient in military equipment—much of which was leftover from the years of U.S. support for the Shah and badly in need of upgrading and parts for repair—Iran had plenty of human bodies to conscript for the war.

And a million Iranian soldiers and civilians were lost in the fight with Iraq. Indeed, a whole martyrology has developed over what Iranians considered a just cause. Those who gave their lives in the fight against Iraq are considered martyrs, and all over the cities in Iran there are large murals on the sides of buildings of young Iranian men who lost their lives in this effort. Iranians don't forget that the U.S. supported Iraq in this effort, nor that Saddam used chemical and biological weapons against their people. To make matters worse, the U.S. shot down an Iranian passenger plane in 1988 over the Strait of Hormuz, killing all 290 passengers and crew aboard.

Hamid Dabashi, an American-Iranian who teaches at Columbia University, argues convincingly that a straight line can be drawn from the CIA-sponsored coup in 1953; through the Islamic Revolution of 1978-79; the overthrow of the Shah; the hostage-taking at the American embassy in Tehran; the Gulf War; the rise of the Taliban, al Qaeda, and Osama bin Laden; to 9-11; and the wars against Afghanistan and Iraq.[18] The Islamic Revolution and the hostage crisis was blowback against the American coup and the years of oppressive rule by the American-backed Shah.

The Soviet Union's occupation of Afghanistan, Iran's neighbor, was a concern to President Reagan in his first term of office. (Reagan called the Soviet Union the "Evil Empire," much like the Ayatollah Khomeini called the United States "The Great Satan." And later, of course, George W. Bush labeled Iran part of the "axis of evil." Demonizing one's political enemies is, of course, a very old trick.) After the Soviet invasion of Afghanistan, the U.S. funded radical guerilla groups called the Mujihideen (Reagan called them "freedom fighters") that paved the way for the emergence of the Taliban.

Perhaps saddest of all is that there were a range of Mujahideen groups, some much more moderate than others, but we backed the most radical groups simply because they were the most brutal and effective in opposing the Soviets. Eventually, the Taliban, also backed by radical Wahabbi Sunnis Arabs from Saudi Arabia, gave safe haven to bin Laden.

Meanwhile, to the West, the U.S. first backed Saddam Hussein in his fight against Iran. But eventually the U.S. adopted a policy of "dual containment" and agreed to supply weapons to Iran to hold in check Saddam's power and ambitions. (Secretary of State Henry Kissinger was quoted as saying, "I hope they kill each other. Too bad they can't both lose.")

Eventually, after the Iran-Iraq War ended in a stalemate, Saddam was emboldened to invade Kuwait, which led to the Gulf War. And bin Ladin was empowered to instigate terrorist attacks against the U.S. and its interests around the world, from the first attack against the World Trade Center in 1993 to an attack against a U.S. military housing complex in Saudi Arabia in 1996, attacks on the U.S. embassies in Kenya and Tanzania in 1998, and the 2000 targeting of the U.S.S. Cole Navy ship in the port of Yemen. Then the big one came: September 11, 2001, the attack which brought down the World Trade Center towers and damaged the Pentagon in Washington, D.C.

Of course it would be the grossest of historical speculation to wonder if 9-11 might never have happened were it not for that American-backed coup against Iran in 1953. Something like it might still have happened, given a resurgent, fundamentalist Islam around the world. Still, one can wonder.

Dabashi says that Iran has still not recovered from the 1953 coup which toppled Prime Minister Mossadeq. The title of Dabashi's book says it well: *Iran: a People Interrupted.* Despite the fact that the U.S. so egregiously violated the sovereignty of Iran and subsequently backed a tyrant like the Shah, after 9-11 Iran expressed some sympathy for the U.S. and provided some assistance in fighting the Taliban in Afghanistan. (I heard nothing but negative comments in Iran about the Taliban. In fact, there is a fear of the Taliban in Iran.)

Then in 2003 Iran sent a proposal to the U.S. through a Swiss intermediary. In exchange for the U.S. ending sanctions against Iran and recognizing Iran has legitimate national security issues, Iran said it was willing to open its nuclear program to inspections, halt its support for Hamas and Islamic Jihad in Palestinian areas, help disarm the Hezbollah in Lebanon, and even move toward recognizing Israel's right to exist. The U.S. didn't even respond, and more recently when asked about it Secretary of State Condaleeza Rice pled ignorance about the proposal. Maybe the Iranian government would never have followed through on their proposal. But how would we ever know if we're not willing to at least talk with them and to negotiate over conflicting and common interests?

Alms boxes are ubiquitous in Iranian cities, a constant reminder that charity is one of the pillars of Islam.

14 State dinner

When countries won't talk to each other, sometimes people or organizations from the hostile countries have opportunities to help open channels of communication and understanding. In political parlance, this is called back-channel or third-party diplomacy.

Such an opportunity fell into our laps early on in our visit to Iran. On our second full day in Iran we were the guests of the Institute for Political and International Studies in Tehran. In the course of our conversation with their leaders, they told us that they'd like to cooperate with MCC in sponsoring two events in Iran: a workshop on peace studies programs; and a roundtable to discuss how religion contributes to both international hostility and peace. Three of our group members were up to the challenge: two who teach in peace studies programs in the United States—University of Notre Dame and Eastern Mennonite University—and a third who serves as MCC liaison to the United Nations. So while we traveled through Iran, they spent time alone working on a response to these proposals.

On the last evening we were in Iran, we went back to the headquarters of the Institute for Political and International Studies. First, four members of our group met with several of their representatives to talk about followup to their proposals. Then the rest of us joined them for what was the finest meal we had had in Iran during our two weeks there. It was the closest thing to a state dinner I'll ever experience.

I was at first seated with other Americans from our tour group. But partway through our meal I was asked to move to another place, as one of the men there was interested in talking with me about the *The Christian Century*. He turned out to be one of the most transparent leaders whom I had encountered there. Currently the director of the school that trains Iran's diplomats, he was interested in hearing about the *The Christian Century* because his father had been a publisher and bookstore owner before the Islamic Revolution. A result of the Revolution was that his father lost everything—his business, his livelihood, and his identity. He also pointed out to me that the devastating Iran-Iraq War took place on the heels of the Iran Revolution. As in many wars, that war had had the effect of concentrating the power in the hands of a few people at the very top. They are still trying to get over that, he pointed out to me, a perspective somewhat at variance with Legenhausen's view of power being widely diffused in the government.

Then my table interlocutor took out a scrap of paper and started drawing a map of the Middle East. Iran, of course, was in the center. And it has one of the largest land masses in all Middle Eastern countries (Saudi Arabia is larger). He asked me, "Of these countries in the Middle East, which ones are democratic?' I suggested Turkey; he demurred a bit, then conceded my point. But he pointed out that Iran is a democratic country, in contrast to many of the other Arab countries around it, or Pakistan to its east. Then he asked, "Why doesn't the United States want to be in diplomatic relations with the largest democratic country in the Middle East?"

I was ready to quibble about how democratic Iran really is. Yes, they have elections, but candidates for the presidency and the parliament are vetted by the Guardian Council, which also must approve all laws passed by the Parliament. And half of the members of the very conservative Guardian Council are chosen by the supreme leader. Besides, democracies involve more than elections: freedom of expression, freedom of the press, the right to assemble, and so forth are essential to democracies.[19] But then I thought that if I challenged Iran's democratic credentials, he might point out to me that the U.S. president is chosen by the electoral college and that the outcome does not necessarily reflect the popular vote; the 2000 election was really settled by the U.S. Supreme Court after some questionable results in the state of Florida. So I didn't go there.

Nevertheless, I pondered his question: Why doesn't our country want to have diplomatic relationships with Iran, democratic or not? Even though our cultures are very different, and our national interests are different, it would be in our self-interest and in the interest of world peace to have diplomatic relationships with Iran.

I was reminded again of my encounter with the ambassador on the flight over to Tehran. When I suggested the source of our national conflict is over a three-letter word, namely *oil*, he responded. "We have oil. We sell you oil. You have planes. You sell us planes." While that sounded too much like the kind of relationship the U.S. had with Iran during the post-World War II era when the Shah was still in power, I took from that a positive. The U.S. and Iran have mutual interests, and with mutual commitment to diplomacy the two countries should be able to work out their differences.

Indeed, in recent years Iran has demonstrated that it has mutual interests with the U.S. and is willing to work with us on them—in the fight against Taliban after 9-11. John W. Limbert, one of the last American diplomats in Iran, also one of the Americans taken hostage, argues that the U.S. should have diplomatic relations with Iran.[20]

One challenge for diplomacy with Iran is that through the 1980s and 1990s the U.S. did not train Persian speaking diplomats, and the older ones retired. It will take some time to train another generation of potential diplomats for Iran. Iran will have some of the same difficulty: There are fewer and fewer people in the country with firsthand knowledge of the U.S.

Limbert says that in negotiating with Iran the U.S. must understand that Iran's first priority is survival and its people see the U.S. as a threat to that objective. Feeling buffeted by hostile forces all around them, they can respond in ways that seem to Westerners irrational at times. And when they hear the U.S. talk about them being part of the "axis of evil" and about regime change, they are convinced that the U.S. intends to overthrow the Islamic Republic. For negotiations to work, the U.S. must reassure them that it won't do anything to destabilize the government, but that in fact the U.S. wants to help them. One of the chief areas of common interest is Iraq. Iran, Limbert says, "shares the American aversion to a divided Iraq, an Iraq dominated by Sunni extremists, or an Iraq under a new version of Saddam Hussein."

The U.S. economic sanctions against Iran aren't having the desired effect. Numerous people in Iran said that they aren't hurting the government but *are* hurting the people, especially with high unemployment and high inflation. Several times too we heard that Iranian companies can no longer get necessary supplies from Western countries, so they have to do business with the Chinese. The result, not surprisingly, is inferior products. The U.S. has a policy of offering Iran mostly "sticks" and few "carrots." This contributes to what political scientists call a "rally round the flag" phenomenon: It means that people who might otherwise resist their government now come to their government's defense. For sure, it discourages the moderates in Iran.

Iran has an authoritarian government, to be sure. Minority religions are marginalized and adherents of the Bahai faith are persecuted. Dissidents—activists, journalists and academics who criticize the government—are squelched. Indeed, they are often imprisoned and sometimes killed. Candidates for office are vetted by the Guardian Council and persons with more democratic convictions are not allowed to run. Women don't have full rights and are often treated as second class citizens. However, Iran is by no means the only authoritarian regime in the world. And we might hope and pray that over time its behavior will change.

Look at Libya as an example. A 1981 *Newsweek* cover called Muammar al-Qaddafi "The Most Dangerous Man in the World," sounding much like accusations more recently of President Ahmadinejad. Yet by 2003 the Libyan dictator announced to the world that he was ending its weapons of mass destruction (WMD) programs—all without any invasion or intervention on the part of outside governments. There was no regime change, but there was behavioral change on the part of the Libyan strong man leader.[21] With patience, hard work, diplomacy, and imagination change like this could come to Iran.

One thing seems clear: War with Iran is not necessary and would be a great tragedy. We found a great deal of pro-American sympathy in Iran, especially among the young people. But as soon as our bombs started falling, all that good will would dissipate. And what repercussions that would set off would be less predictable and controllable than even those set in motion by the overthrow of Saddam Hussein.[22]

These young women believe it will take a long time for better relationships to be forged between Muslims and Christians.

15 Father Abraham

Not having adjusted to the time change yet in our first week in Iran, I awoke early one morning in the holy city of Qom. I could hear the call to prayers at the local mosque and a rooster crowing—right in the city. I was reminded of being in a very different world from where I normally live. Then I checked the clock on my PDA, which has a world map showing where in the world it is daylight at any given time. Just at the time I checked it, the whole world was under darkness, except eastern Asia and Australia were in daylight and the sun was just about to rise on Iran.

Our light—the sun—does come out of the East, and it is from the light that we get our source of orientation—hence, we refer to the East as the Orient. And we Christians claim that Jesus is the light, he who came out of the Middle East, which is neither strictly East nor West, yet somehow both Eastern and Western. I also had to think about how all the major religions of the world came out of either the East or the Middle East, including the three Abrahamic religions. Why is it that we in the West feel we are the enlightened ones, when so much of our religious light has come from somewhere else?

A day earlier we had visited the Center for Interreligious Dialogue, which is part of Iran's Organization for Islamic Guidance and Communication. There we were introduced to Professor Rasoul Rasoulipour, who offered his vision for interreligious dialogue and understanding.[23] All the Abrahamic religions share a belief in one God, he maintained, even though we follow different paths toward the ultimate reality. Anyone who submits to the will of God is a Muslim, according to the Qur'an. Indeed, if there is only one God, then there is only one religion, one way of submitting to the will of God. This perspective created some cognitive dissonance for me. While I believe that there is only one God and that Jews, Christians, and Muslims worship the same God despite our different understandings of this God, it seemed to me to flatten out the differences between the three Abrahamic religions to say that in essence there really is only one religion.[24]

In the ancient and beautiful city of Esfahan, we bumped into three young Muslim women who, like so many, asked why we were visiting their country. Our American leader said to them, "We are here to work toward better relationships between Muslims and Christians." Without hesitation, one of the Iranian women piped up, "That's going to take a long time."

How right she was. But this should not keep us from trying. Consider how many of the hot spots in the world involve hostile relationships between two or more of the Abrahamic faiths. Not only is world peace at stake. As an Islamic professor in Qom indicated, what a witness it would be to the rest of the world if the Abrahamic faiths could get along with each other.

One evening in Qom after our group had visited an American couple studying there, we all needed a ride back to our hotel across town. It was cold and snowy; in fact, Iran had more snow that week than they had had in fifty years. I imagined we'd have to stand out in the cold to wait for cabs to go back to our rooms. But instead Mohammad Ali Shomali, a philosopher professor who was also a guest at the American couple's apartment that night, offered us rides home, even though he had to make several trips through the treacherous, snowy streets. It was a wonderful expression of Iranian and Muslim hospitality.

The very next morning Professor Shomali was our lecturer. He talked about Christian-Muslim relationships, Catholic-

Muslim dialogue in England that he is engaged in, and the fact he had specifically studied Christianity during a sabbatical in England. In his study of Christianity, he said, he wasn't "looking for our rivals, but our long lost cousins." He also admonished us that there is no way to show respect for Muslims without showing respect for Islam. (Wouldn't we say the same thing about ourselves in relation to Christianity?) Christians and Muslims should work together on mutual concerns such as the environment, peace, and the meeting of human need. What about Christians supporting a mosque, or Muslims a church? he wondered.

Indeed, there is work that Christians and Muslims can do, some of which is theological work. Islam has a place for Jesus in the Qur'an—Jesus is a great prophet—yet Christians have no similar place for Islam in their Scriptures or theology. This causes a problem for Muslims. But the place that Muslims have for Jesus—son of Mary but not Son of God—is obviously not the same place Christians have for him. This causes a problem for Christians. This theological conundrum should keep us busy for awhile. But it is necessary and important work. And like the young woman in Esfahan said, "It's going to take a long time," so we should get on with it right away.

We have two tasks: One is to learn about Islam and the different branches of the Islamic faith. We can read about Islam, but better still is learning to know Muslims who practice it on a daily basis. The other task is for Christians to talk with each other about how we regard Islam. Many Christians have learned—through many mistakes, hard work, and conversations with Jews—how to make a place for Judaism; that work still remains in our relationship with Islam and Muslims.

Evie Shellenberger told our group about an encounter she had had with a Muslim while studying in Qom. The Shellenbergers and their neighbor friends dropped in on another family for a meal. But there was a misunderstanding, and the host family was not expecting them. Still, they were welcomed into the home and a wonderful meal was served despite the mistake.

After the meal the hosts wondered why the Shellenbergers had chosen to live in Iran. The host family was surprised to learn that the Shellenbergers were Mennonites, not Muslims. Immediately they wanted to know about the Mennonites. While Evie was trying to frame her response in the Farsi she was learning, Heidi, her Muslim friend, began to passionately and respectfully explain Mennonite convictions and practices— about their desire for peace and attempt at living simple lives.

Later Evie reflected on this experience:

> I have wondered if perhaps one important outcome of interfaith dialogue, Muslims and Christians journeying together, is that the "other" will indeed know us and make us known to others as we would like to be known. This is exactly what Heidi did for me. And it was a powerful moment for me. Would I . . . make her faith be known in a way that she would want to be known? Would I be able to speak passionately and kindly about the strengths of another's faith?[25]

There is a time and a place for talking about the weaknesses and failures of another group or religion. Too often, though, we compare our strengths with the weaknesses of another religion, our ideals with the realities of another religion. We haven't earned the right to judge another group or person before we have actually come to truly know the other in a deep and personal way.

*This white dove appeared as a sign of hope on a fountain after
our tour group went through the Hasrat-e Masumeh mosque,
the spiritual center of Qom and a Shiite holy cite. Fatemeh, the
Imam Reza's sister, is buried here.*

16 Home again

The week after I got back from Iran I went to see my chiropractor. He said he was surprised to see me. He thought I'd never get out of Iran, that he'd never see me again, and that he might as well archive my records. He was partly being facetious, but only partly so. He seemed genuinely concerned about my well-being while traveling in Iran. In any case, my worst fear—that the U.S. would bomb Iran while our group was there and that, in turn, we'd be taken as hostages—didn't happen. I never really worried about it while there.

Of course it doesn't matter too much what my chiropractor thinks of Iran. But the U.S. government's stance toward Iran is another matter. Will the U.S. choose to engage Iran through diplomacy and cultural exchanges? Or will it use force to try to impose its will on Iran as it did in the 1953 coup?

President Obama's approach to Iran is hopeful. Already in the 2008 primaries, he indicated a desire to engage Iran, rather than simply place sanctions upon them or, worse, bomb them. His stance at that time was ridiculed by his political opponents. Perhaps most hopeful of all was his June 2009 address to the Muslim world in Cairo, Egypt, in which he acknowledged American involvement in the 1953 overthrow of President Mossedeq. To my knowledge, it is unprecedented for an American president to acknowledge that the American government has been involved in the overthrow of another sovereign country's government. But as the Muslim world said in response to Obama's speech: It was only words that must be followed up with actions.

Engaging Iran will not be easy and will require patience. The suspicions between the two countries run deep. And as Limbert has argued, Iranians have a different style of negotiations, a style that can appear opaque to Western forms of reasoning and dialogue. How much patience does the U.S. have? President Obama will be under enormous pressure at home and in Israel to take some kind of military action against Iran if it appears as though Iran will persist in its nuclear enrichment program, which for a variety of reasons it no doubt will, not least of which is national pride in defiance of western powers.

Nevertheless, Iranian government leaders have said on numerous occasions that they have no intention of creating nuclear weapons and that, in fact, the developing of nuclear weapons goes against Islam. Is "Christian America" prepared to say that the development of nuclear weapons goes against Christianity? The U.S. has not been "fair and balanced" when it tries to prevent other countries from developing nuclear weapons. The U.S. has one of the largest nuclear weapon stockpile in the world and is the only country ever to have used them on another country. There again, Obama may have some leverage, given the fact he has said his desire is to see a world free of nuclear weapons.

The U.S. needs to assure Iran that it has no intentions of working at regime change in Iran, even though it might wish for some change in how this regime runs its affairs.[26] So many interventions into Middle Eastern countries by the U.S. and other Western governments grew out of ignorance of these strange and foreign countries, the Iraq War being the most recent example. Minimally, we need to get to know these countries, their people and culture, their history and religions. That is why I chose to tour Iran. And that is why I've committed my stories and learning to print.

Most of all, I want my experience to be a witness to my conviction that followers of Jesus should not let their government dictate to them who their enemies are. As we found out so many times in Iran, the people of Iran aren't our enemies; they want to be our friends. To be sure, we have enemies, people who want to do us harm. And it may just be that the government of Iran would like to do us harm. But just as we shouldn't let our government tell us who these enemies are, we shouldn't let them dictate how we should regard or relate to our enemies. We may appear naïve at times, but we should make every effort possible to engage our enemies. In so doing, we may "disarm" our enemies—nonviolently.

Afterword

Two years after my visit to Iran tensions are higher than ever within the country and between Iran and the West.

In June 2009 Ahmadinejad was reelected president in what many claim was a rigged election. The Interior Ministry claimed he had received over sixty-two percent of the vote, but some calculate he may have gotten no more than a fourth of eligible votes. People took to the streets in protest, spawning a Green Movement in opposition to the current leadership. As Hamid Dabashi, Iranian professor at Columbia University, has written, unlike previous generations of Iranian protesters, they are not now asking "Where is my gun" but "Where is my vote?" Subsequently, periodic protests have led to crackdowns, with some protesters being killed or imprisoned and subjected to sham trials. It is reported also that China is supplying Iran with armed, anti-protest vehicles similar to ones China used to squelch the Tiennamen Square revolt.

Iran's nuclear program also appears to be more extensive than assumed several years ago. Some believe that they might attain the capacity to build a nuclear weapon as early as 2010. The launching of a longer-range rocket that could reach Israel and even farther exacerbated the tensions in the region and with Western countries. Will Israel be able to resist the temptation to bomb Iran's purported nuclear sites, despite the fact that they are likely buried deep in the ground and could not be fully destroyed? Military action against Iran would most likely set back the Green Movement for years, if not kill it entirely. Western countries are talking about additional sanctions against Iran, but it isn't clear how sanctions can be targeted at the leadership without making life more difficult for the people themselves.

In this tense environment I've heard from several of my Iranian contacts. They are clearly quite anxious about their future. They express deep longings for peace. And they request our prayers as sons and daughters of our common spiritual ancestor, Father Abraham.

Who can say what the future holds for Iran, its people, and its relationships with the rest of the world? Will it be a tragic one? Or can we hope for something better? Indeed, we must pray for them—and for us. And we must continue to find ways of being in solidarity of the people of Iran to support their aspirations for peace, for freedom and for more open relationships with the rest of the world.

Appendix I:
Eight Points About Iran's
Nuclear Program

1. The U.S. government's National Intelligence Estimate reported in November 2007 that Iran halted its nuclear weapons program in fall 2003. Iran is developing the capacity to enrich uranium, as it is entitled to do under the Nuclear Nonproliferation Treaty. International inspectors have found no evidence of an actual nuclear weapons program.

2. U.S. national intelligence officials have testified that Iran would need several years to develop nuclear weapons capability. Ample time is available to craft an effective diplomatic strategy to prevent nuclear weaponization.

3. The U.S. government is working with European countries and international agencies such as the International Atomic Energy Agency (IAEA) and the UN Security Council. Cooperative diplomacy is an effective strategy for encouraging compliance with nonproliferation goals. Iran reportedly restrained its nuclear program in 2003 in response to increasing international scrutiny, pressure and incentives.

4. U.S. differences with Iran should be resolved through diplomacy, not unilateral sanctions and military threats, which have strengthened the hand of conservatives within Iran and led to further isolation of Iranian reformers.

5. A major goal of U.S. policy should be to maintain and increase Iran's cooperation with the IAEA, so that international inspectors continue to have access to Iranian nuclear facilities and can detect any prohibited activities. Most of what we know about the Iranian nuclear program has come from IAEA inspectors on the ground.

6. Iran cooperated with international inspectors in a special program to clarify questions about its past nuclear activities. In 2008 IAEA officials reported "good progress" in resolving previous uncertainties about Iran's nuclear program.

7. Senior Iranian officials have said that Tehran is prepared to negotiate and might allow an international consortium to enrich uranium in Iran. The U.S. should enter into high-level discussions with Iran, without preconditions. Washington should offer incentives to Tehran, such as the lifting of nonmilitary sanctions, to encourage greater Iranian cooperation in denuclearization and regional stabilization efforts.

8. Nonproliferation objectives in Iran should be linked to broader denuclearization efforts. The United States and other nuclear-weapons states have signed the nonproliferation treaty with Iran and more than 180 other countries, pledging to take measures to achieve nuclear disarmament. The U.S. would be in a stronger position to prevent nuclear proliferation by others if it fulfilled its own commitment to negotiate for disarmament.

—*David Cortright is Director of Policy Studies at the Kroc Institute for International Peace Studies at the University of Notre Dame.*

Appendix II:
Jesus and the Shi'a
Savior—Waiting for
the Mahdi

When Iran president Mahmoud Ahmadinejad addressed an open letter to George W. Bush in May 2006, he invoked Judgment Day, the day when the deeds of all political leaders will be examined. Ahmadinejad asked Bush whether either of them would be accepted "in the promised world, where . . . Jesus Christ (Peace Be Upon Him) will be present." Ahmadinejad appeared to be trying to connect with American Christians and to critique Bush in light of the U.S. president's own faith. He expressed not only his own reverence as a Muslim for Jesus but his expectation that Jesus would return to earth.

This expectation is part of a Muslim belief in the appearance of the Mahdi—a savior who, along with Jesus, is expected to bring justice and peace to the world at the end of this age. Belief in the Mahdi plays a special role in Shi'a Islam, a strand of Islam which includes about 15 percent of Muslims worldwide. Shi'as predominate in Iran and account for more than half the Muslims in Iraq and Lebanon. Significant Shi'a pockets also exist in Kuwait, Pakistan, Azerbaijan, Turkey and Syria, forming a Shi'a crescent, a potential power bloc that worries many Sunni Muslims as well as Western powers.

Shi'a Islam arose in disagreements over who should succeed the Prophet Muhammad when he died in 632. Shi'as believe that it should have been Ali, the Prophet's cousin and the husband of his daughter, Fatima. Ali was highly regarded for his pious character and spiritual leadership. But Muhammad was succeeded by Abu Bakr, and then by Umar and Uthman. These first three caliphs were mainly political and military rulers. As Shi'as tell it, by 656, when Uthman died and Muslim rule extended into eastern Iran, Armenia, Syria and Egypt, upper-class Muslims had become obsessed with power and wealth. They looked down on their new subjects, even those who had become Muslim. This empire had strayed far from the simpler, more brotherly and righteous society prescribed by Muhammad.

In 656 Ali became the fourth caliph of Islam, but he was murdered in 661, and the Caliphate passed to Uthman's descendants, the Umayyads. This precipitated the most significant event in Shi'a history. In 680 Ali's son Husayn (Muhammad's grandson) and 72 of his followers were surrounded by a massive Umayyad force at Karbala, in what is now Iraq. Despite the hopeless odds, Husayn fought back, but he and his followers were killed.

According to many Shi'as, Husayn undertook his desperate battle because Muslims had strayed so far from Muhammad's teaching that only the shocking murder of his grandson would jolt them into realizing the error of their ways. Shi'as mourn Husayn's death on their most holy day, Ashoura. Their extensive weeping for his sacrifice and their prayers to obtain its atoning benefits have been compared to the rituals by which Christians mark Good Friday. But remembrance of Husayn's martyrdom also prompts vows to avenge him.

Shi'as believe that Muslims should always have had one leader who combines administrative skills and spiritual ones, as Muhammad and Ali did. Shi'as call these extraordinary persons imams. (In Sunni Islam, the term imam refers to a leader of a mosque.) For Shi'as, Ali was the first imam and Husayn the third.

Iranian Shi'as count 12 imams. All or most of them, according to Shi'a tradition, were murdered by powerful Muslim governments. Although Shi'as have ruled Iran since 1501, through most of their history Shi'as have been a minority group, otherwise excluded from centers of power. They believe that Allah took the twelfth imam, Abu'l-Qasim Muhammad, into "occultation"—that is, Allah hid and protected him—in about 874. It is he who will reappear as the Mahdi, and Jesus will reappear with him.

Some Sunni Muslims also await a Mahdi, though they usually expect him to be a contemporary who will suddenly proclaim himself as such. Some Sunnis did so in the past and led armies against their enemies (such as Muhammad Ahmad in the Sudan, who succeeded in ending Egyptian occupation in 1881-1885). But Iranian Shi'as await someone who has long represented a people persecuted ever since Muhammad's time and who will finally vindicate them.

Since Iran is the world's leading Shi'a power, many Iranians expect that it will play a major role in preparing for the Mahdi and in his subsequent activity. This belief renders Iranian Mahdism enormously significant in global politics.

What do Iranian Shi'as expect to happen when their Mahdi, or twelfth imam, and Jesus reappear? It is impossible to give a definite answer, because Iranian Shi'as differ among themselves. I have spoken at two large Mahdism conferences in Tehran and dialogued formally with Shi'a leaders several times. My impression is that Iranian Mahdism could either lead toward political and military expansion or be channeled into cooperative efforts.

Iranian leaders valorize the 1979 revolution that overthrew the Shah and brought Ayotollah Khomeini to power. Khomeini often invoked Shi'a history and compared his cause with Husayn's and the Shah's with the Umayyads, Husayn's killers.

When he took power, Khomeini executed many of his opponents. Khomeini also began exporting the Shi'a revolution. He kindled discontent in other countries, sometimes with violent means or violent results, until Iran was exhausted by its war with Iraq (1980-1988). Iran might have lost that war had not many thousands of young people, heeding the Shi'a call to martyrdom, stormed Iraqi forces with few weapons or none at all.

Though Iran's recent history raises the possibility of a militant form of Islam, Mahdism can also be invoked to encourage interfaith and international dialogue. This is because Mahdism, like all eschatologies, envisions more than the conquest of evil; it envisions the coming of a just and peaceful social order and the end of poverty and suffering for all peoples. A major question is whether the future is seen as discontinuous or continuous with the preceeding history. When eschatologies stress discontinuity, they often legitimate efforts to bring about that future by violent means. When eschatologies emphasize some measure of continuity, they usually inspire people to start living by the ideals of the future in the present, and to try to realize them in their societies. One can see this element also among Iranian Shi'as, who believe that becoming more righteous, individually and socially, is a prerequisite for the Mahdi's coming. Many Iranians and their leaders regard this as the special task of the world's only Shi'a-governed nation.

Though Shi'a Islam and Christianity both have eschatological visions, and this opens an avenue for dialogue between Iranian Shi'as and North American Christians, one difference between Shi'a and Christian eschatology is the central role of Shari'a law in Mahdism. Iranians insist that the Mahdi will ensure justice for all, but in Iran today, Shari'a law is sometimes implemented by the lash, by amputation or by hanging. Women are subjected to various restrictions (for example, all women, both residents and visitors, must wear headscarves in public).

But many interpretations of Shari'a flourish in the Muslim world and in Iran. For example, Shirin Ebadi, the 2003 Nobel

Peace Prize laureate, who is greatly honored by many Iranians (and opposed by others), repeatedly invokes Islamic legal tradition to support women's rights and other human rights.

Jesus' place in Mahdism provides another matter for discussion. Jesus often appears to be the Mahdi's second in command. The Muslims I have talked to leave Jesus' role vague. When I asked a Shi'a scholar how the Mahdi's coming would affect Christians, he said that there would be no problems, since Jesus and the Mahdi will work together. I pressed on: "What if these Christians believe Jesus is divine?" Jesus, he replied, will clarify that he is not divine and that he was Muhammad's forerunner. "What if Jesus says he is what we Christians believe?" I asked. The scholar stared and stammered; that possibility was incomprehensible—the Jesus who comes with the Mahdi will be the honored prophet, nothing more.

Following a recent conference in Tehran I spent ten days in Iran. While there I was repeatedly interviewed for radio, television, and films and constantly asked for my views of Christianity and America. Many interviewers, mostly young people, kept asking questions well beyond the allotted time. Iranians seem desperate for contacts with Americans. They want to hear what we really think, and for us to hear what they really think. In view of the ominous clouds that overhang American-Iranian relations, I hope that we will continue to develop and learn from such conversations.

—*Thomas Finger is an independent scholar who is involved in ecumenical and interfaith work with the Mennonite Church U.S.A., Mennonite World Conference, and Mennonite Central Committee.*

Appendix III: Iran Timeline

1906-11: Constitutional Revolution

1921-41: Reign of Reza Shah Pahlavi

1934: Establishment of Tehran University, a modern, secular institution

1936: Banning of the veil in public by the Reza Shah

1941: Abdication of rule by Reza Shah, son Muhammed Reza Shah installed in his place

1941-45: WW II occupation of Iran by Britain, Soviet Union and U.S.

1951: Muhammed Mossadeq, a nationalist, elected prime minister

1952: Iranian oil nationalized

1953: CIA engineers overthrow of Prime Minister Mossadeq

1953: Muhammed Reza Shah Iran reinstated with U.S. backing

1954: Anglo-Iranian Oil Company (later becomes British Petroleum [BP]) leads international cartel that controls Iran oil production

1957: With U.S. and Israeli help, Shah forms secret police (SAVAK) to monitor and quell dissidents

1963: Shi'a uprising put down by the Shah; Ayatollah Khomeini emerges as unchallenged leader of Iranian Shi'a community

1964: Ayatollah Khomeini, who opposes Shah and U.S., goes into exile

1971: The Shah's opulant celebration at Persepolis of the purported 2,500 year anniversary of the Persian monarchy

1973: OPEC oil embargo, led by the Shah, then Arab-Israeli War, increases gas price dramatically

1978-79: Islamic Revolution begins

1979: Shah flees country; Ayatollah Khomeini returns from exile

1979: American hostages taken at embassy, held for 444 days

1980: Iraq attacks Iran, U.S. backs Iraq

1981: American hostages released after Reagan inauguration

1982: Iran rejects favorable ceasefire agreement from Iraq

1985: Iran-Contra affair (clandestine sale of arms to Iran to fund Contras in Nicaragua)

1988: UN brokers ceasefire in Iraq-Iran war

1988: U.S. guided missile shoots down an Iranian passenger plane

1989: Khomeini orders death of Salman Rushdie, author of *The Satanic Verses*

1989: Khomeini dies, Khamenei replaces him as Supreme Leader

1997: Reform-minded Khatami elected president

1998-99: Iran rejects Clinton administration's offer of roadmap to better relations

2001-02: Iran cooperates with U.S. action against Taliban in Afghanistan

2003: U.S. ignores Iran proposal to open negotiations about nuclear program and Middle East peace

2003: Iran consents to enhanced inspection of its nuclear program

2005: Hardliner Ahmadinejad elected president

2006: Iran suspends participation in inspection program

2006-2007: UN Security Council imposes targeted sanctions on Iran

2007: National Intelligence Estimate (NIE) reports that Iran suspended its nuclear bomb program in 2003

2009: Ahmadinejad reelected president in what some consider a rigged outcome; protests ensue.

Notes

1. See Richard A. Kauffman, "Inside Iran: First-person Encounters," *The Christian Century* 125, no. 12 (June 17, 2008): 22-26.

2. For this idea of conscripting others' stories for our purposes, I'm indebted to Rowan Williams, *Writing in the Dust: After September 11* (Grand Rapids, Mich.: Eerdmans, 2002), 63-73.

3. Miroslav Volf, *Exclusion & Embrace: A Theological Exploration of Identity, Otherness, and Reconciliation* (Nashville, Tenn.: Abingdon, 1996), 250-253.

4. I recognize this is my way of phrasing the problem. Official Iranian response would be to refer to it as the "Zionist problem." However, as Laurie Pierce has pointed out to me, "Over the last few years official Iranian government rhetoric has shifted from demanding a one-state solution to accepting 'any solution the Palestinians accept,' which implies that Iran would be more open than in the past to accepting a two-state solution and possibly recognizing Israel."

5. Michael Axworthy, *A History of Iran: Empire of the Mind* (New York: Basic Books, 2008), xiii. In personal correspondence, Laurie Pierce pointed out to me, "Attendance at Friday prayers does not have nearly the importance in Shi'a Islam that it does in Sunni, and in neither branch of Islam is it as integral a part of the believer's spiritual experience and religious life as church attendance is and has historically been for Christians. In modern Iran it's simply not indicative of religiosity, and so I think it's misleading to compare it to church attendance. In Qom we knew many clerics who hadn't attended Friday prayers in months or even years."

6. From their perspective, the United States is a young upstart, the one causing mischief in their (Middle Eastern) neighborhood.

7. Hamid Dabachi, *Iran: A People Interrupted* (New York: New Press, 2007).

8. Afshin Molavi. *The Soul of Iran: A Nation's Journey to Freedom* (New York, N.Y.: W. W. Norton & Company, 2002), 139.

9. Shirin Ebadi, *Iran Awakening: A Memoir of Revolution and Hope*

119

(New York: Random House, 2006), 147.

10. Ed Martin, "MCC and Iran," *Peace Office Newsletter* 31, no. 3 (July-September 2001), 1-3.

11. From "Field Guide for MCC Program in Qom."

12. Roy Hange, "A Dialogue of Civilizations," in *Borders* and *Bridges: Mennonite Witness in a Religiously Diverse World*, ed. Peter Dula and Alain Epp Weaver (Telford, Pa.: Cascadia Publishing House, 2007), 110.

13. Maren Tyedmars Hange and Roy Hange, "Dislocated for Service," *Peace Office Newsletter* 31, no. 3 (July-September 2001): 3-6.

14. Roy Hange, "Give Us This Day...," *Peace Office Newsletter* 31, no. 3 (July-September 2001): 11.

15. Ahmadinejad has tried to clarify that he is not completely dismissing the reality of the Holocaust, only the magnitude of it, and that he doesn't want to liquidate all Israelis, just the current form of its government, comparing it to the ending of the Soviet Union as it once existed.

16. Andrew Burke and Mark Elliott, *Iran*, 5th. ed. (Oakland, Calif.: Lonely Planet, 2008), 52.

17. Marguerite Del Giudice. "Persia: Ancient Soul of Iran," *National Geographic* (August 2008), 14-67; with photographs by Newsha Tavakolian; includes a map.

18. Hamid Dabashi, *Iran: A People Interrupted* (New York: The New Press, 2007), 137ff.

19. A helpful resource for understanding structure and functions of the very complex Iranian government is the BBC web site noted in the resource section.

20. John W. Limbert, "Negotiating with the Islamic Republic of Iran" (United States Institute of Peace Special Report 199, January 2008), at www.usip.org/pubs/specialreports/sr199.html

21. Robert S. Litwak, "Regime Change 2.0: There is more than one way to get a rogue state to change its ways," *Wilson Quarterly* (Autumn 2008): 22-27.

22. See "The Folly of Attacking Iran," preface to a new edition of Stephen Kinzer, *All the Shah's Men: An American Cop and the Roots of Middle East Terror* (Hoboken, N.J.: John Wiley, 2008), ix-xxiii. In this preface, which is worth the price of the book, Kinzer argues that the consequences of the U.S. bombing Iran would likely be to turn the very unpopular leaders of Iran into heroes of resistance; give them a reason to launch attacks against American interests around the world; strengthen Iranian nationalism and Shiite aggression and recruit more Muslims for extremism; weaken the democratic forces in Iran and sour pro-American Iranians toward the U.S.; put off real political change in Iran for at least another generation; commit the U.S. to involvement in the Middle East for years to come; enrage the Shiite led government in Iraq on whom the U.S. depends for a resolution to that Iraq War; and possibly disrupt the flow of oil.

23. Professor Rasoulipour spent the summer of 2008 at the University

of Notre Dame because of his interest in Alvin Plantinga, a philosopher who teaches at Notre Dame. I bumped into him and his wife shopping at a Kohl's department store in Mishawaka, Ind., of all places, and we had a friendly conversation. I invited him to come to Chicago to visit us, but unfortunately he didn't make it.

24. Laurie Pierce has subsequently helped me to understand the professor's point in cultural context: "Talking about 'one religion' is rooted in the Islamic conception of revelation. For Muslims it's not so much a flattening of differences as it is a viewing of the Abrahamic faiths through the lens of progressive revelation. Muslims often use the 'one religion' concept in good faith to acknowledge and build common ground in the early stages of dialogues and relationships with people of other religions. Focusing on differences at the outset of the conversation would be rude in Iranian culture."

25. From Evie Shellenberger's journal, which she graciously shared with me. Heidi, by the way, is Professor Legenhausen's Iranian wife.

26. Iran was on the verge of elections when I was finishing up this manuscript. As we now know, hardliner Ahmadinejad did win reelection amid protests, but demographics are on the side of Iran becoming a more open society, given the youthful population and the fact many of them are open to Western influences.

Further Resources

Books on Iran

Bird, Christiane. *Neither East Nor West: One Woman's Journey through the Islamic Republic.* New York: Washington Square Press, 2002.

Burke, Andrew and Mark Elliott. *Iran,* 5th. ed. Oakland, Calif.: Lonely Planet Publications, 2008.

Cole, Juan. *Sacred Space and Holy War: The Politics, Culture and History of Shi`ite Islam.* London, England: I. B. Taurus, 2005.

Dabashi, Hamid. *Iran: A People Interrupted.* New York: New Press, 2007.

Dula, Peter and Alain Epp Weaver, editors. *Borders and Bridges: Mennonite Witness in a Religiously Diverse World.* Telford, Pa.: Cascadia Publishing House, 2007. See chapter 7, Roy Hange, "A Dialogue of Civilizations: The Encounter of Iranian Shi'ites and North American Mennonites," pp. 105-116.

deBellaigue, Christopher. *In the Rose Garden of the Martyrs: A Memoir of Iran.* New York: Harper Collins, 2004.

*Dumas, Firoozeh. *Funny in Farsi: A Memoir of Growing Up Iranian in America.* New York: Random House, 2004.

*Dumas, Firoozeh. *Laughing Without an Accent: Adventures of an Iranian American, at Home and Abroad.* New York: Villard, 2008.

Ebadi, Shirin, with Azadeh Moaveni. *Iran Awakening : One Woman's Journey to Reclaim Her Life and Country.* New York: Random House, 2007.

Keddie, Nikki R. *Modern Iran: Roots and Results of Revolution,* updated ed. New Haven, Connecticut: Yale University Press, 2003.

The Firoozeh Dumas' books aren't about Iran. Rather, they're about an Iranian immigrant family living in the United States. Dumas is a very funny writer.

Kinzer, Stephen. *All the Shah's Men: An American Coup and the Roots of Middle East Terror,* with a new preface. Hoboken, N.J.: John Wiley & Sons, 2008.

Molavi, Afshin. *The Soul of Iran: A Nation's Journey to Freedom.* New York: W. W. Norton, 2002.

Nasr, Seyyed Hossein. *Islam: Religion, History, and Civilization.* San Francisco, Calif.: HarperSanFrancisco, 2007.

Parsi, Trita. *Treacherous Alliance: The Secret Dealings of Israel, Iran, and the U.S.* New Haven, Connecticut: Yale University Press, 2007.

Pierce, Laurie. *What Is Iran?* Scottdale, Pa.: Herald Press, 2009.

Sanasarian, Eliz. *Religious Minorities in Iran.* Cambridge, England: Cambridge University Press, 2000.

Shomali, Mohammad Ali. *Discovering Shi'I Islam,* 6th. ed. London, England: Institute of Islamic Studies, 2007.

Ward, Terence. *Searching for Hassan: a Journey to the Heart of Iran.* New York: Anchor Books, 2002.

Wright, Robin. *The Last Great Revolution: Turmoil and Transformation in Iran.* New York: Vintage, 2001.

Magazines

The following are thematic issues devoted to coverage of Iran:

The Christian Century 125, no. 12 (June 17, 2008).

National Geographic 214, no. 2 (August 2008).

Online resources

www.un.org/Depts/Cartographic/map/profile/iran.pdf
United Nations map of Iran set within the region

www.usip.org/pubs/specialreports/sr199.html
Paper by John W. Limbert, one of the last American diplomats in Iran and one of the hostages taken in 1979, in which he argues that the U.S. should enter into negotiations with Iran, despite the challenges involved.

http://news.bbc.co.uk/2/shared/spl/hi/middle_east/03/iran_power/html/default.stm The BBC's excellent chart and description of Iran's very complicated government structure

http://hrw.org/reports/2008/iran0108/
A Human Rights Watch report, "You Can Detain Anyone for Anything," on "Iran's Broadening Clampdown on Independent Activism"

http://www.worldpublicopinion.org/pipa/articles/brmiddleeast-
    nafricara/468.php?lb=brme&pnt=468&nid=&id=
Results of a public opinion poll in Iran measuring attitudes toward the
    U.S. and relationships between the two countries on such matters as
    the nuclear issue and Iraq

www.thethoughtfulchristian.com
Three-part study guide on the people, history, culture, politics, and reli-
    gion of Iran, written by Richard A. Kauffman with a leader's guide by
    Megan Pillow Davis. Can be bought for $14.00 and then freely pho-
    tocopied and distributed for study groups.

Iranian films

Iran has a rich cinema tradition, despite restrictions place on it by the Islamic government. The following, all available at www.netflix.com, are especially recommended:

Baran. Revelatory insights into the tension between Iranians and "illegal"
    Afghan immigrants that reminds Americans of our own immigration
    tensions.

Children of Heaven. Delightful story about how a brother and sister share
    one pair of shoes and cover for each other in the process of avoiding
    shame.

Under the Moonlight. An Islamic seminarian discovers his true vocation
    when, after being robbed by a youthful thief, he discovers an under-
    world of poor, homeless people.

Persepolis. An animated film based on Marjane Satrapi's autobiographical
    graphic novel about her childhood in Iran, her youth in France, and
    her return to Iran as an adult.

Acknowledgments

This book would never have come to fruition without the support of my employer, *The Christian Century*. I'm grateful to John M. Buchanan, editor/publisher, and to David Heim, executive editor, for making it possible for me to go on a learning tour of Iran, which served as the basis of this book.

When old friends Evie and Wally Shellenberger heard of my interest in their learning tour through Iran, they made sure that I got what was apparently the last berth with their tour group. In their retirement the Shellenbergers dared what most retirees would eschew: they moved to Qom, Iran, as exchange students through Mennonite Central Committee. Their love and passion for the culture and people of Iran was palpable. I thank them for pushing me to see the good of the country, not just its obvious problems and weaknesses.

A benefit of traveling with an educated, alert group of people was experiencing a new culture with many ears and eyes besides my own. Along the way we had invaluable discussions about what we were observing and experiencing in Iran. My fellow travelers included Bertha Beachy, retired missionary and bookstore manager; James Cooper, student at Indiana University; David Cortright, from the Fourth Freedom Forum and the Kroc Institute for International Peace Studies at the University of Notre Dame; Rebecca Fast and Paul Shetler, then both Goshen College students; Gwen Gustafson-Zook, staff at

MCC Great Lakes; Doug Hostetter, MCC liaison to the United Nations; Rachel Spory, recent graduate from Eastern Mennonite University; and Dan Wessner, then political science professor at EMU and now at the University of Denver.

Beachy's years of living in Somalia helped us to better understand Islam. Cortwright's experience at the Kroc Institute and as former executive director of SANE (Committee for a Sane Nuclear Policy) helped put into perspective the controversial positions Iran's government has taken in the development of nuclear materials. Along with Beachy and Cortwright, Hostetter and Wessner are both savvy internationalists and travelers, helping us to see things in geopolitical perspective. Gustafson-Zook helpfully raised issues about the role and treatment of women in Iran. And the students kept issues about human rights in the country on the front burner.

There were numerous people in Iran who helped make our trip a success, but I want to single out the following: Mr. Haghani, our Iranian-based tour guide, gracefully and patiently smoothed out the inevitable rough edges on a tour like this, not the least of which was the fact that while we were there Iran had more snow than in any year for the last fifty. American-born Muhammad Legenhausen, who has made Iran his home, helped me to look for God in the Iranian people and served as an excellent host, bridging the gap between the United States and Iran, Christianity, and Islam. On several snowy nights while we were in Qom, David Wolfe and LindaKusse-Wolfe welcomed us into their apartment for a meal. They were at the time exchange students in Qom.

Wally Shellenberger and Laurie Pierce (author of *What Is Iran?* by Herald Press and a former exchange student in Iran) were gracious enough to read my manuscript. I thank them for their feedback.

Two friends may be surprised to see their names here: Frances Ringenberg and Cindy Crosby. Both knew I was working on this book, and at critical junctures when my inspiration and willpower were languishing they encouraged me to keep on.

Finally, but certainly not last, my thanks to Suzanne, my life's companion. She indulges my wanderlust and encourages my endeavors.

In going to Iran I saw myself as part pilgrim, part student and part journalist in Iran. In this last role I went to Iran to see and experience what I could see and then report to others what I had learned and experienced, without being beholden to anyone. That is what I have tried to do in this small book. No one else, therefore, can be blamed for its content. The culpability rests with me.

The Author

Richard A. Kauffman grew up in Lancaster County, Pennsylvania. He has degrees from Hesston and Goshen colleges and graduate degrees from Eastern Baptist (now Palmer) Theological Seminary, Princeton Theological Seminary, and Temple University.

Currently senior editor and book review editor for *The Christian Century* magazine, he has also served as an editor at Mennonite Publishing House and *Christianity Today* and is senior editor of *Leader* magazine. Additionally, he was administrative vice president and instructor in theology at Associated Mennonite Biblical Seminary. He has been a conference youth pastor and has pastored several Mennonite congregations in New Jersey and Ohio.

Kauffman and his wife Suzanne have two adult children and three grandchildren. They're members of Lombard (Ill.) Mennonite Church. Suzanne is co-manager of a Ten Thousand Village store in Glen Ellyn, Illinois, where they live.

CPSIA information can be obtained
at www.ICGtesting.com
Printed in the USA
FFOW02n1328220514
5476FF

9 781931 038751